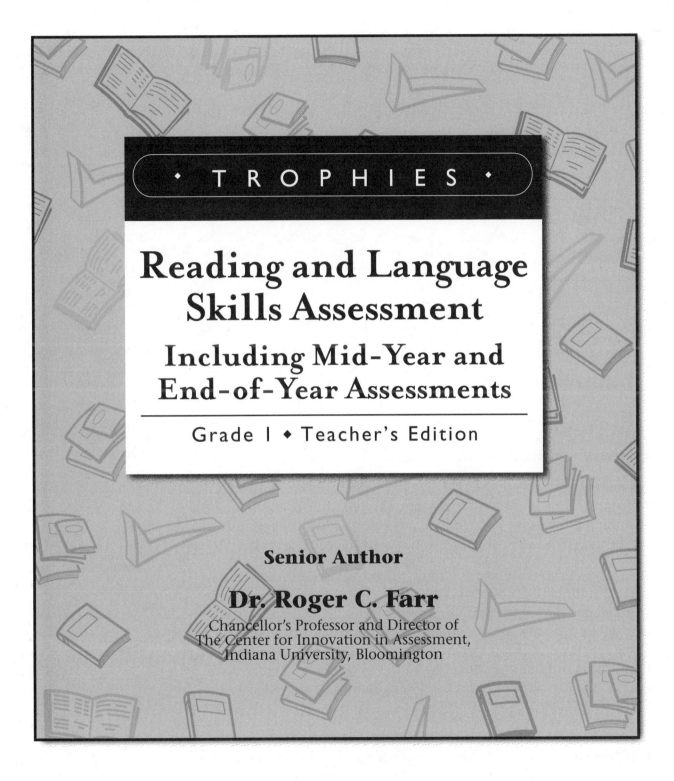

# · TROPHIES ·

# Reading and Language Skills Assessment

## Including Mid-Year and End-of-Year Assessments

Grade 1 • Teacher's Edition

**Senior Author**

## Dr. Roger C. Farr

Chancellor's Professor and Director of
The Center for Innovation in Assessment,
Indiana University, Bloomington

# Harcourt

Orlando   Boston   Dallas   Chicago   San Diego

Visit *The Learning Site!*

**www.harcourtschool.com**

Printed in the United States of America

ISBN 0-15-324961-7

8 9 10   170   10 09 08 07 06 05 04

# Table of Contents

· · · · · · · · · · · · · · · · · · · · · · · · · · · · · · · · · · · · · · · · · · · · · · · · · · · · · · · · · ·

# Appendix

• • • • • • • • • • • • • • • • • • • • • • • • • • • • • • • • • • • • • • • • • • • • • • • •

# Trophies
# Assessment Components

••••••••••••••••••••••••••••••••••••••••••••••••••••••••••••

The chart below gives a brief overview of the assessment choices that are available at this grade. The titles in boldface can be found in this Teacher's Edition.

| **Entry-Level Assessments** | **To plan instruction** |
| --- | --- |
| *Placement and Diagnostic Assessments* | ◆ To determine the best placement for a student and to assess strengths and weaknesses |
| ***Reading and Language Skills Pretests*** | ◆ To determine a student's proficiency with selected skills *before* starting instruction |
| **Formative Assessments** | **To monitor student progress** |
| *End-of-Selection Tests* | ◆ To monitor a student's comprehension of each selection and selection vocabulary |
| *Oral Reading Fluency Assessment* | ◆ To monitor the rate and accuracy with which a student reads text aloud |
| Assessment notes at "point of use" in the Teacher's Edition | ◆ To monitor selected skills and strategies as they are taught |
| ***Mid-Year Reading and Language Skills Assessment*** | ◆ To monitor how well a student has retained reading and language skills |
| **Summative Assessments** | **To assess mastery of skills taught** <br> **To assess ability to apply skills and strategies** |
| ***Reading and Language Skills Posttests*** | ◆ To assess mastery of reading and language skills taught in a theme |
| *Holistic Assessment* | ◆ To evaluate a student's ability to apply reading and writing skills and strategies to new situations |
| ***End-of-Year Reading and Language Skills Assessment*** | ◆ To evaluate mastery of reading and language skills taught during the year |

# Overview of the Teacher's Edition

· · · · · · · · · · · · · · · · · · · · · · · · · · · · · · · · · · · · · · · · · · · · · · · · · · · · · · ·

This Teacher's Edition is organized into two major sections. Each section contains information about a separate assessment component. The two assessment components are as follows:

## *Reading and Language Skills Assessments*

Two parallel forms of the *Reading and Language Skills Assessments*, a Pretest and a Posttest, are available for each theme at this grade. These assessments evaluate the specific skills taught in the themes. The assessments can be used in tandem before and after instruction in the theme, or they can be used independently. For example, only the posttest could be used to evaluate how well students learned the skills taught in a particular book.

## *Mid-Year* and *End-of-Year Skills Assessments*

Two cumulative assessments are also included in this Teacher's Edition. The *Mid-Year Reading and Language Skills Assessment* evaluates the skills taught in Books 1-1, 1-2, and 1-3. The *End-of-Year Reading and Language Skills Assessment* evaluates the skills taught in Books 1-1 through 1-5.

Copying masters for all of the assessment booklets are located in the Appendix. They are organized as follows:

*Guess Who*/Book 1-1 *Reading and Language Skills Assessment*
*Catch a Dream*/Book 1-2 *Reading and Language Skills Assessment*
*Here and There*/Book 1-3 *Reading and Language Skills Assessment*
*Mid-Year Reading and Language Skills Assessment*

*Time Together*/Book 1-4 *Reading and Language Skills Assessment*
*Gather Around*/Book 1-5 *Reading and Language Skills Assessment*
*End-of-Year Reading and Language Skills Assessment*

Harcourt • Reading and Language Skills Assessment

# Reading and Language Skills Assessments

## Description of the Assessments

The *Reading and Language Skills Assessments* are criterion-referenced tests designed to measure students' achievement on the skills taught in each of the themes. Criterion-referenced scores help teachers make decisions regarding the type of additional instruction that students may need.

Five *Reading and Language Skills Assessments* are available at this grade level— one assessment for each theme. The assessments evaluate students' achievement in decoding/phonics, vocabulary, research and information skills, comprehension, and language. The formats used on the *Reading and Language Skills Assessments* follow the same style as those used in instruction. This ensures that the assessments are aligned with the instruction.

## Scheduling the Assessments

The *Reading and Language Skills Assessments* have been designed to correlate with specific skills introduced and reinforced within each theme of the program. Therefore, a *Reading and Language Skills Assessment Pretest* could be administered before a book is started to determine which skills need to be emphasized. Or, a *Reading and Language Skills Assessment Posttest* could be administered after a book is completed to verify that students can apply the skills that were taught.

If possible, a *Reading and Language Skills Assessment* should be given in one session. The pace at which you administer the assessment will depend on your particular class and group. The assessments are not timed. Most students should be able to complete an assessment in about thirty minutes.

## General Guidelines for Administering

- Write each child's name on a booklet before distributing the assessment booklets; or, if you prefer, distribute the booklets and have children write their names on the Name line.

- When administering an assessment, speak in a natural tone, pacing directions so that all children have time to answer. Repeat or clarify items that children do not hear or directions that they do not understand. Directions that should be read verbatim to children are printed in *italic* type. Directions that are for your information only (not to be read to children) are printed in regular type.

- Some of the subtests (e.g., Decoding/Phonics) involve pronouncing letter sounds. In the Specific Assessment Directions, letter sounds are enclosed with two slash marks, such as /s/, /p/, or /t/. It is important to avoid distorting the pronunciation of individual sounds. For example, /b/ should not be pronounced as 'buh." Instead, pronounce it in a loud whisper, without using your vocal cords.

- Each subtest (e.g., Decoding, Vocabulary, Comprehension) begins with a sample item to familiarize children with the test format. Have children fold the assessment booklet so that only the page they are working on is facing up. Demonstrate on the board how to fill in answer circles by drawing three answer circles and filling in one of them. Then go through the sample item with the class, making sure every child understands what to do and how to mark the answers. Explain to children that if they change their minds after filling in an answer circle, they should erase their marks completely and then fill in the answer circle they do want. Make sure they understand that they are to fill in only one answer circle for each question.

- Monitor children closely as you administer an assessment, making sure that children are on the correct page and item and that they are marking their answers correctly.

- Accommodations can be made for children with special needs (e.g., special education, ESL). If accommodations are made for a child, they should be noted in the space provided on the cover of the assessment booklet.

- Prior to administering an assessment, the following general directions could be read to the children.

**Say:** *Today you will be answering questions about some of the things we have learned together in class. Do your very best and try to answer each of the questions.*

- Tell children to work until they come to the word "STOP." When they come to the word "STOP," they should put their pencils down and wait until the class is ready to begin the next subtest.

# Specific Directions for Administering the *Reading and Language Skills Assessment*

∙∙∙∙∙∙∙∙∙∙∙∙∙∙∙∙∙∙∙∙∙∙∙∙∙∙∙∙∙∙∙∙∙∙∙∙∙∙∙∙∙∙∙∙∙∙∙∙∙∙∙∙∙∙∙∙∙∙∙∙∙∙∙∙∙∙

### *Guess Who*/Book 1-1: PRETEST

### DECODING/PHONICS: *Vowels*

**Objective: Identify and isolate the medial phoneme of a spoken word (short vowels)**

**Say:** *Put your finger by the Sample. Look at the three pictures. I will tell you a sound to listen for. Then I will name the three pictures while you listen carefully. Choose the picture that has the sound I tell you. Which picture has the /a/ sound? rope? can? geese? Fill in the answer circle under the picture that has the /a/ sound.* Pause while children mark their answers.

Then **say:** *Which picture has the /a/ sound?* Call on a child to provide the correct answer.

Then **say:** *Yes, **can** has the /a/ sound. You should have filled in the answer circle under the picture of the **can**. If you did not fill in the correct answer circle, erase your mark completely and fill in the answer circle under the picture of the **can**.*

Make sure that children have filled in the correct answer circle. Provide help for children who have difficulty.

Then **say:** *Now you will look at some more pictures and choose the pictures that have the sounds I tell you. Fill in the answer circle under the pictures you choose. If you change your mind after you have marked your answer, erase your mark and fill in the answer circle under the picture you do want.*

Continue the test following the same procedures, first having children listen for a specific phoneme, and then having them find the picture that has that phoneme.

**Say:**

1. *Which picture has the /a/ sound? poke? bike? cat?*
2. *Which picture has the /a/ sound? cap? ice? goat?*
3. *Which picture has the /i/ sound? soap? sit? cake?*
4. *Which picture has the /i/ sound? flake? glue? rip?*
5. *Which picture has the /o/ sound? face? stop? hike?*
6. *Which picture has the /o/ sound? hop? fly? tack?*

### DECODING/PHONICS: *Vowels*

**Objective: Read decodable words with short vowels**

**Say:** *Put your finger on the picture of **dad** in the Sample. Next to the picture you see three words in a row. Find the word that names the picture. Which word is **dad**? Fill in the answer circle under the word **dad**.* Pause while children mark their answers.

Then **say:** *Which word is **dad**?* Call on a child to provide the correct answer.

Then **say:** *Yes, the first word in the row is **dad**, and it names the picture. You should have filled in the answer circle under the first word, **dad**. If you did not fill in the correct answer circle, erase your mark completely and fill in the answer circle under the first word, **dad**.*

Make sure that children have filled in the correct answer circle. Provide help for children who have difficulty.

Then **say**: *Now you will look at some more pictures and fill in the answer circle under the word that names each picture. If you change your mind after you have marked your answer, erase your mark and fill in the answer circle under the word you do want.*

Continue the test following the same procedures, having children find the word that names each picture.

**Say:**

7. *Find the picture of* **sip**. *Which word is* **sip**? *Fill in the answer circle under the word* **sip**.

8. *Find the picture of a* **hill**. *Which word is* **hill**? *Fill in the answer circle under the word* **hill**.

9. *Find the picture of a* **sack**. *Which word is* **sack**? *Fill in the answer circle under the word* **sack**.

10. *Find the picture of a* **man**. *Which word is* **man**? *Fill in the answer circle under the word* **man**.

11. *Find the picture of a* **top**. *Which word is* **top**? *Fill in the answer circle under the word* **top**.

12. *Find the picture of a* **lock**. *Which word is* **lock**? *Fill in the answer circle under the word* **lock**.

### DECODING: Digraphs

**Objective: Recognize sound-letter relationships of digraphs**

In administering this subtest, do not say the sound the letters make or name the letters for the children.

**Say**: *Put your finger by the sample. Look at the two letters. Next to the letters you see three pictures. I will name the three pictures for you. Choose the picture whose name ends with the sound the letters stand*

for. *Look at the Sample. Which picture name ends with the sound those letters stand for? map? sack? bed? Fill in the answer circle under the picture name that* **ends** *with the sound the letters stand for.* Pause while children mark their answers.

Then **say**: *Which picture name ends with same sound the letters stand for in the sample?* Call on a child to provide the correct answer.

Then *say*: *Yes,* **sack** *ends with the same sound the letters stand for in the sample. You should have filled in the answer circle under the picture of the* **sack**. *If you did not fill in the correct answer circle, erase your mark and fill in the answer circle under the picture of the* **sack**.

Make sure that children have filled in the correct answer circle. Provide help for children who have difficulty.

Then **say**: *Now you will look at some more pictures and choose the picture names that have the sound the letters stand for. Fill in the answer circle under the pictures you choose. If you change your mind after you have marked your answer, erase your mark and fill in the answer circle under the picture you do want.*

Continue the test following the same procedures, first having children look at the letters, and then having them find the picture names that end with the sound those letters stand for.

**Say:**

13. *Look at the letters. Which picture name ends with the sound the letters stand for? chick? egg? pin?*

14. *Look at the letters. Which picture name ends with the sound the letters stand for? bat? kick? man?*

15. *Look at the letters. Which picture name ends with the sound the letters stand for? lock? tub? jam?*

Harcourt • Reading and Language Skills Assessment

**16.** *Look at the letters. Which picture name ends with the sound the letters stand for? hop? moon? tack?*

## COMPREHENSION: Sequence

### Objective: Recognize sequence of events

**Say:** *Put your finger by the Sample at the top of the page. Find the short story called "Growing a Plant." We will read the story together. Follow along while I read the story aloud.*

> **Here is how to grow a plant.**
>
> **Put the plant in the sun.**
>
> **Give the plant a drink every day.**
>
> **Watch the plant grow.**

Then **say:** *Find the question under the Sample story. Follow along while I read the question aloud. What should you do first? Watch the plant grow? Put the plant in the sun? Give the plant a drink?* Call on a child to provide the correct answer.

Then **say:** *Yes, first you should **Put the plant in the sun.** Fill in the answer circle by **Put the plant in the sun.*** Pause while children mark their answers.

Make sure that children have filled in the correct answer circle. Provide help for children who have difficulty.

Then **say:** *Now we will read two more stories together. After we read each story, you will answer some questions about the story. Listen carefully and follow along as I read the story aloud. The first story is called "Cam Makes a Snack."*

> **Cam helped her friend make a snack.**
>
> **First, her friend put ice cream in two bowls.**
>
> **Then, Cam put nuts on the ice cream.**
>
> **Last, Cam and her friend sat down to eat their snack.**

Then **say:** *Follow along while I read the questions aloud. Question 17 says:*

> **What did the friend do <u>first</u>?**
>
> **She put ice cream in two bowls.**
>
> **She put nuts on the ice cream.**
>
> **She had a drink.**

*Fill in the answer circle in front of the answer that tells what the friend did **first**.*

Pause for children to mark their answers.

Then **say:** *Now follow along while I read the next question aloud. Question 18 says:*

> **What did Cam and her friend do <u>last</u>?**
>
> **They put nuts on the ice cream.**
>
> **They put ice cream in two bowls.**
>
> **They sat down to eat their snack.**

*Fill in the answer circle in front of the answer that tells what Cam and her friend did last.* Pause for children to mark their answers.

Then **say:** *Now we will read another story together. Listen carefully and follow along as I read the story aloud. The second story is called "Beth and Dan."*

> **Beth and Dan were reading a book.**
>
> **First, they read about a kangaroo.**
>
> **Next, they read about a hippo.**
>
> **Last, they read about a tiger.**
>
> **Beth and Dan had fun reading.**

Then **say:** *Follow along while I read the questions aloud. Question 19 says:*

> **What did Beth and Dan read about <u>first</u>?**
>
> **a hippo**
>
> **a kangaroo**
>
> **a tiger**

Harcourt • Reading and Language Skills Assessment

*Fill in the answer circle in front of the answer that tells what Beth and Dan read about **first**.* Pause for children to mark their answers.

Then **say**: *Follow along while I read question 20 aloud. Question 20 says:*

**What did Beth and Dan read about <u>last</u>?**

**a hippo**

**a kangaroo**

**a tiger**

*Fill in the answer circle in front of the answer that tells what Beth and Dan read about **last**.* Pause for children to mark their answers.

### LANGUAGE

**Objective: Recognize correct word order; recognize asking and telling sentences; recognize naming parts of sentences**

**Say:** *Put your finger by Sample 1. You see some words with **Yes** and **No** under them. I will read the words to you. Decide whether the words are in the correct order to make a sentence. The words by Sample 1 say:*

**my cat? Where is**

*If the words are in the correct order to make a sentence, fill in the answer circle under **Yes**. If the words are not in the correct order to make a sentence, fill in the circle under **No**.* Pause while children mark their answers.

Then **say**: *Are the words in the correct order to make a sentence?* Call on a child to provide the correct answer.

Then **say**: *No, the words are not in the correct order. You should have filled in the answer circle under **No**. If you did not fill in the correct answer circle, erase your mark completely and fill in the answer circle under **No**.*

Make sure that children have filled in the correct answer circle. Provide help for children who have difficulty.

Then **say**: *Now I will read you some more words. If the words are in the correct order to make a sentence, fill in the answer circle under **Yes**. If the words are not in the correct order, fill in the answer circle under **No**. If you change your mind after you have marked your answer, erase your mark and fill in the answer circle you do want.*

Continue the test following the same procedures, having children determine whether the words are in the correct order to make a sentence. Pause after reading each question so that children can mark their answers.

**Say:**

21. *The words in this row say: **I see a red apple**. Fill in the answer circle under **Yes** or **No**.*

22. *The words in this row say: **big surprise. Look at my** Fill in the answer circle under **Yes** or **No**.*

Tell children to find sample 2. **Say:** *Put your finger by Sample 2. You see a sentence with a period and a question mark under it. I will read the sentence to you. Decide whether it is a telling or an asking sentence The sentence in Sample 2 says:*

**Will you come now**

*Is that a telling or an asking sentence? Fill in the answer circle under the period if **Will you come now** is a telling sentence. Fill in the answer circle under the question mark if **Will you come now** is an asking sentence.* Pause while children mark their answers.

Then **say**: *Is **Will you come now** a telling or an asking sentence?* Call on a child to provide the correct answer.

Then **say**: *Yes, **Will you come now** asks a question. You should have filled in the answer circle under the question mark.*

*If you did not fill in the correct answer circle, erase your mark completely and fill in the answer circle under the question mark.*

Make sure that children have filled in the correct answer circle. Provide help for children who have difficulty.

Then **say**: *Now I will read you some more sentences. Choose the correct end mark for each sentence. If you change your mind after you have marked your answer, erase your mark and fill in the answer circle you do want.*

Continue the test following the same procedures, having children determine the end mark for each sentence. Pause after reading each question so that children can mark their answers.

**Say:**

**23.** *The sentence in this row says*: **The jam is good.** *Choose the correct end mark.*

**24.** *The sentence in this row says*: **Where is my snack** *Choose the correct end mark.*

Tell children to find Sample 3. **Say:** *Put your finger by Sample 3. You see a sentence. I will read the sentence to you. Decide what is the naming part of the sentence. The sentence in Sample 3 says:*

**I went with him.**

*What is the naming part of the sentence? Fill in the answer circle under* **I** *if* **I** *is the naming part of the sentence. Fill in the answer circle under* **went with him** *if* **went with him** *is the naming part of the*

*sentence. Pause while children mark their answers.*

Then **say**: *What is the naming part of the sentence?* Call on a child to provide the correct answer.

Then **say**: *Yes,* **I** *is the naming part of the sentence. You should have filled in the answer circle under* **I**. *If you did not fill in the correct answer circle, erase your mark completely and fill in the answer circle under* **I**.

Make sure that children have filled in the correct answer circle. Provide help for children who have difficulty.

Then **say**: *Now I will read you some more sentences. Choose the naming part for each sentence. If you change your mind after you have marked your answer, erase your mark and fill in the answer circle you do want.*

Continue the test following the same procedures, having children determine the naming part for each sentence. Pause after reading each question so that children can mark their answers.

**Say:**

**25.** *The sentence in this row says*: **My mom is here.** *Choose the naming part.*

**26.** *The sentence in this row says*: **The lamp is lit.** *Choose the naming part.*

After all children have completed this subtest, **say**: *We have finished this activity.* Collect the assessment booklets.

# Specific Directions for Administering the *Reading and Language Skills Assessment*

## *Guess Who*/Book 1-1: POSTTEST

### DECODING/PHONICS: *Vowels*

**Objective: Identify and isolate the medial phoneme of a spoken word (short vowels)**

**Say:** *Put your finger by the Sample. Look at the three pictures. I will tell you a sound to listen for. Then I will name the three pictures while you listen carefully. Choose the picture that has the sound I tell you. Which picture has the /a/ sound? rope? can? geese? Fill in the answer circle under the picture that has the /a/ sound.* Pause while children mark their answers.

Then **say:** *Which picture has the /a/ sound?* Call on a child to provide the correct answer.

Then **say:** *Yes,* **can** *has the /a/ sound. You should have filled in the answer circle under the picture of the* **can**. *If you did not fill in the correct answer circle, erase your mark completely and fill in the answer circle under the picture of the* **can**.

Make sure that children have filled in the correct answer circle. Provide help for children who have difficulty.

Then **say:** *Now you will look at some more pictures and choose the pictures that have the sounds I tell you. Fill in the answer circle under the pictures you choose. If you change your mind after you have marked your answer, erase your mark and fill in the answer circle under the picture you do want.*

Continue the test following the same procedures, first having children listen for a specific phoneme, and then having them find the picture that has that phoneme.

Say:

1. *Which picture has the /a/ sound? bat? hill? bed?*
2. *Which picture has the /a/ sound? mitt? bell? fan?*
3. *Which picture has the /i/ sound? man? dig? sun?*
4. *Which picture has the /i/ sound? pin? ham? leg?*
5. *Which picture has the /o/ sound? fish? rock? mug?*
6. *Which picture has the /o/ sound? top? pan? gift?*

### DECODING/PHONICS: *Vowels*

**Objective: Read decodable words with short vowels**

**Say:** *Put your finger on the picture of* **dad** *in the Sample. Next to the picture you see three words in a row. Find the word that names the picture. Which word is* **dad**? *Fill in the answer circle under the word* **dad**. Pause while children mark their answers.

Then **say:** *Which word is* **dad**? Call on a child to provide the correct answer.

Then **say:** *Yes, the first word in the row is* **dad**, *and it names the picture. You should have filled in the answer circle under the first word,* **dad**. *If you did not fill in the correct answer circle, erase your mark completely and fill in the answer circle under the first word,* **dad**.

Make sure that children have filled in the correct answer circle. Provide help for children who have difficulty.

Harcourt • Reading and Language Skills Assessment

Then **say:** *Now you will look at some more pictures and fill in the answer circle under the word that names each picture. If you change your mind after you have marked your answer, erase your mark and fill in the answer circle under the word you do want.*

Continue the test following the same procedures, having children find the word that names each picture.

**Say:**

7. *Find the picture of a **lip**. Which word is **lip**? Fill in the answer circle under the word **lip**.*

8. *Find the picture of **sit**. Which word is **sit**? Fill in the answer circle under the word **sit**.*

9. *Find the picture of a **hat**. Which word is **hat**? Fill in the answer circle under the word **hat**.*

10. *Find the picture of a **map**. Which word is **map**? Fill in the answer circle under the word **map**.*

11. *Find the picture of a **fox**. Which word is **fox**? Fill in the answer circle under the word **fox**.*

12. *Find the picture of a **sock**. Which word is **sock**? Fill in the answer circle under the word **sock**.*

### DECODING: *Digraphs*

#### Objective: Recognize sound-letter relationships of digraphs

In administering this subtest, do not say the sound the letters make or name the letters for the children.

Then **say:** *Put your finger by the sample. Look at the two letters. Next to the letters you see three pictures. I will name the three pictures for you. Choose the picture whose name ends with the sound the letters stand for. Look at the Sample. Which picture name ends with the sound those letters stand for? map? sack? bed?*

*Fill in the answer circle under the picture name that **ends** with the sound the letters stand for.* Pause while children mark their answers.

Then **say:** *Which picture name ends with the same sound the letters stand for in the sample?* Call on a child to provide the correct answer.

Then *say: Yes, **sack** ends with the same sound the letters stand for in the sample. You should have filled in the answer circle under the picture of the **sack**. If you did not fill in the correct answer circle, erase your mark and fill in the answer circle under the picture of the **sack**.*

Make sure that children have filled in the correct answer circle. Provide help for children who have difficulty.

Then **say:** *Now you will look at some more pictures and choose the picture names that have the sound the letters stand for. Fill in the answer circle under the pictures you choose. If you change your mind after you have marked your answer, erase your mark and fill in the answer circle under the picture you do want.*

Continue the test following the same procedures, first having children look at the letters, and then having them find the picture names that end with the sound those letters stand for.

**Say:**

13. *Look at the letters. Which picture name ends with the sound the letters stand for? rope? crab? rock?*

14. *Look at the letters. Which picture name ends with the sound the letters stand for? sock? ship? frog?*

15. *Look at the letters. Which picture name ends with the sound the letters stand for? bed? tack? hot?*

16. *Look at the letters. Which picture name ends with the sound the letters stand for? stop? swim? chick?*

Harcourt • Reading and Language Skills Assessment

## COMPREHENSION: Sequence

**Objective: Recognize sequence of events**

**Say:** *Put your finger by the Sample at the top of the page. Find the short story called "Growing a Plant." We will read the story together. Follow along while I read the story aloud.*

> **Here is how to grow a plant.**
>
> **Put the plant in the sun.**
>
> **Give the plant a drink every day.**
>
> **Watch the plant grow.**

Then **say:** *Find the question under the Sample story. Follow along while I read the question aloud. What should you do first? Watch the plant grow? Put the plant in the sun? Give the plant a drink?* Call on a child to provide the correct answer.

Then **say:** *Yes, first you should* **Put the plant in the sun.** *Fill in the answer circle by* **Put the plant in the sun.** *Pause while children mark their answers.*

Make sure that children have filled in the correct answer circle. Provide help for children who have difficulty.

Then **say:** *Now we will read two more stories together. After we read each story, you will answer some questions about the story. Listen carefully and follow along as I read the story aloud. The first story is called "Dress Up."*

> **First, Liz put on Mom's hat.**
>
> **Then, she put on Mom's coat.**
>
> **The hat and coat were too big!**
>
> **Last, Liz laughed at how she looked.**

Then **say:** *Follow along while I read the questions aloud. Question 17 says: What did Liz do* <u>first</u>?

> **She put on Mom's coat.**
>
> **She put on Mom's hat.**
>
> **She laughed at how she looked.**

*Fill in the answer circle in front of the answer that tells what Liz did* **first.** *Pause for children to mark their answers.*

Then **say:** *Now follow along while I read the next question aloud. Question 18 says: What did Liz do* <u>last</u>?

> **She put on Mom's coat.**
>
> **She put on Mom's hat.**
>
> **She laughed at how she looked.**

*Fill in the answer circle in front of the answer that tells what Liz did last. Pause for children to mark their answers.*

Then **say:** *Now we will read another story together. Listen carefully and follow along as I read the story aloud. The second story is called "Going Fishing."*

> **Dad and Jake wanted to go fishing.**
>
> **First, Jake dug up some worms.**
>
> **Next, he put the worms in a can.**
>
> **He showed the can of worms to Dad.**
>
> **Last, Jake and Dad went fishing.**

Then **say:** *Follow along while I read the questions aloud. Question 19 says: What did Jake do* <u>first</u>?

> **He put worms in a can.**
>
> **He went fishing with Dad.**
>
> **He dug up some worms.**

*Fill in the answer circle in front of the answer that tells what Jake did* **first.** *Pause for children to mark their answers.*

Then **say:** *Follow along while I read question 20 aloud. Question 20 says: What did Jake do* <u>last</u>?

> **He put worms in a can.**
>
> **He and Dad went fishing.**
>
> **He showed the can of worms to Dad.**

Harcourt • Reading and Language Skills Assessment

*Fill in the answer circle in front of the answer that tells what Jake did **last**.* Pause for children to mark their answers.

### LANGUAGE

**Objective: Recognize correct word order; recognize asking and telling sentences; recognize naming parts of sentences**

**Say:** *Put your finger by Sample 1. You see some words with **Yes** and **No** under them. I will read the words to you. Decide whether the words are in the correct order to make a sentence. The words by Sample 1 say:*

**my cat? Where is**

*If the words are in the correct order to make a sentence, fill in the answer circle under **Yes**. If the words are not in the correct order to make a sentence, fill in the circle under **No**.* Pause while children mark their answers.

Then **say**: *Are the words in the correct order to make a sentence?* Call on a child to provide the correct answer.

Then **say**: *No, the words are not in the correct order. You should have filled in the answer circle under **No**. If you did not fill in the correct answer circle, erase your mark completely and fill in the answer circle under **No**.*

Make sure that children have filled in the correct answer circle. Provide help for children who have difficulty.

Then **say**: *Now I will read you some more words. If the words are in the correct order to make a sentence, fill in the answer circle under **Yes**. If the words are not in the correct order, fill in the answer circle under **No**. If you change your mind after you have marked your answer, erase your mark and fill in the answer circle you do want.*

Continue the test following the same procedures, having children

determine whether the words are in the correct order to make a sentence. Pause after reading each question so that children can mark their answers.

Say:

**21.** *The words in this row say: **Pam said she will come**. Fill in the answer circle under **Yes** or **No**.*

**22.** *The words in this row say: **little fish. I see a** Fill in the answer circle under **Yes** or **No**.*

Tell children to find Sample 2. **Say:** *Put your finger by Sample 2. You see a sentence with a period and a question mark under it. I will read the sentence to you. Decide whether it is a telling or an asking sentence. The sentence in Sample 2 says:*

**Will you come now**

*Is that a telling or an asking sentence? Fill in the answer circle under the period if **Will you come now** is a telling sentence. Fill in the answer circle under the question mark if **Will you come now** is an asking sentence.* Pause while children mark their answers.

Then **say**: *Is **Will you come now** a telling or an asking sentence?* Call on a child to provide the correct answer.

Then **say**: *Yes, **Will you come now** asks a question. You should have filled in the answer circle under the question mark. If you did not fill in the correct answer circle, erase your mark completely and fill in the answer circle under the question mark.*

Make sure that children have filled in the correct answer circle. Provide help for children who have difficulty.

Then **say**: *Now I will read you some more sentences. Choose the correct end mark for each sentence. If you change your mind after you have marked your answer, erase your mark and fill in the answer circle you do want.*

Harcourt • Reading and Language Skills Assessment

Continue the test following the same procedures, having children determine the end mark for each sentence. Pause after reading each question so that children can mark their answers.

**Say:**

**23.** *The sentence in this row says:* **Here is your bike** *Choose the correct end mark.*

**24.** *The sentence in this row says:* **Do you like mints** *Choose the correct end mark.*

Tell children to find sample 3. **Say:** *Put your finger by Sample 3. You see a sentence. I will read the sentence to you. Decide what is the naming part of the sentence. The sentence in Sample 3 says:*

**I went with him.**

*What is the naming part of the sentence? Fill in the answer circle under* **I** *if* **I** *is the naming part of the sentence. Fill in the answer circle under* **went with him** *if* **went with him** *is the naming part of the sentence.* Pause while children mark their answers.

Then **say:** *What is the naming part of the sentence?* Call on a child to provide the correct answer.

Then **say:** *Yes,* **I** *is the naming part of the sentence. You should have filled in the answer circle under* **I**. *If you did not fill in the correct answer circle, erase your mark completely and fill in the answer circle under* **I**.

Make sure that children have filled in the correct answer circle. Provide help for children who have difficulty.

Then **say:** *Now I will read you some more sentences. Choose the naming part for each sentence. If you change your mind after you have marked your answer, erase your mark and fill in the answer circle you do want.*

Continue the test following the same procedures, having children determine the naming part for each sentence. Pause after reading each question so that children can mark their answers.

**Say:**

**25.** *The sentence in this row says:* **You may see it.** *Choose the naming part.*

**26.** *The sentence in this row says:* **My cat likes milk.** *Choose the naming part.*

After all children have completed this subtest, **say:** *We have finished this activity.* Collect the assessment booklets.

Harcourt • Reading and Language Skills Assessment

# Specific Directions for Administering the *Reading and Language Skills Assessment*

••••••••••••••••••••••••••••••••••••••••••••••••••••••••••

### *Catch a Dream*/Book 1-2: PRETEST

### *DECODING: Vowels*

**Objective: Identify and isolate the medial phoneme of a spoken word (short and *R*-controlled vowels)**

**Say:** *Put your finger by Sample 1. Look at the three pictures. I will tell you a sound to listen for. Then I will name the three pictures while you listen carefully. Choose the picture that has the sound I tell you. Which picture in Sample 1 has the /e/ sound? net? mug? pig? Fill in the answer circle under the picture that has the /e/ sound.* Pause while children mark their answers.

Then **say:** *Which picture has the /e/ sound?* Call on a child to provide the correct answer.

Then **say:** *Yes, **net** has the /e/ sound. You should have filled in the answer circle under the picture of **net**. If you did not fill in the correct answer circle, erase your mark completely and fill in the answer circle under the picture of **net**.*

Make sure that children have filled in the correct answer circle. Provide help for children who have difficulty.

**Say:** *Now put your finger by Sample 2. Look at the three pictures. I will tell you a sound to listen for. Choose the picture that has the sound I tell you. Which picture in Sample 2 has the /ôr/ sound? swim? sled? corn? Fill in the answer circle under the picture that has the /ôr/ sound.* Pause while children mark their answers.

Then **say:** *Which picture has the /ôr/ sound?* Call on a child to provide the correct answer.

Then **say:** *Yes, **corn** has the /ôr/ sound. You should have filled in the answer circle under the picture of **corn**. If you did not fill in the correct answer circle, erase your mark completely and fill in the answer circle under the picture of **corn**.*

Make sure that children have filled in the correct answer circle. Provide help for children who have difficulty.

Then **say:** *Now you will look at some more pictures and choose the pictures that have the sounds I tell you. Fill in the answer circle under the pictures you choose. If you change your mind after you have marked your answer, erase your mark and fill in the answer circle under the picture you do want.*

Continue the test following the same procedures, first having children listen for a specific phoneme, and then having them find the picture that has that phoneme.

**Say:**

1. *Which picture has the /e/ sound? light? hole? bed?*
2. *Which picture has the /e/ sound? tie? desk? gate?*
3. *Which picture has the /u/ sound? bus? swim? sheep?*
4. *Which picture has the /u/ sound? chick? feet? run?*
5. *Which picture has the /ôr/ sound? kick? fork? shell?*
6. *Which picture has the /ôr/ sound? store? ship? cap?*

## DECODING: Vowels

**Objective: Read decodable words with short and *R*-controlled vowels**

Say: *Put your finger on the picture of the **pet** in Sample 1. Next to the picture you see three words in a row. Find the word that names the picture. Which word is **pet**? Fill in the answer circle under the word **pet**.* Pause while children mark their answers.

Then **say**: *Which word is **pet**?* Call on a child to provide the correct answer.

Then **say**: *Yes, the first word in the row is **pet**, and it names the picture. You should have filled in the answer circle under the first word, **pet**. If you did not fill in the correct answer circle, erase your mark completely and fill in the answer circle under the first word, **pet**.*

Make sure that children have filled in the correct answer circle. Provide help for children who have difficulty.

Say: *Put your finger on the picture of the stork in Sample 2. Look at the picture and the three words in that row. Find the word that names the picture. Which word is **stork**? Fill in the answer circle under the word **stork**.* Pause while children mark their answers.

Then **say**: *Which word is **stork**?* Call on a child to provide the correct answer.

Then **say**: *Yes, the second word in the row is **stork**, and it names the picture. You should have filled in the answer circle under the second word, **stork**. If you did not fill in the correct answer circle, erase your mark completely and fill in the answer circle under the second word, **stork**.*

Make sure that children have filled in the correct answer circle. Provide help for children who have difficulty.

Then **say**: *Now you will look at some more pictures and fill in the answer circle under the word that names each picture. If you change your mind after you have marked your answer, erase your mark and fill in the answer circle under the word you do want.*

Continue the test following the same procedure, having children find the word that names each picture.

**Say:**

7. *Find the picture of a **mess**. Which word is **mess**? Fill in the answer circle under the word **mess**.*
8. *Find the picture of **ten**. Which word is **ten**? Fill in the answer circle under the word **ten**.*
9. *Find the picture of a **nut**. Which word is **nut**? Fill in the answer circle under the word **nut**.*
10. *Find the picture of **stuck**. Which word is **stuck**? Fill in the answer circle under the word **stuck**.*
11. *Find the picture of a **horn**. Which word is **horn**? Fill in the answer circle under the word **horn**.*
12. *Find the picture of **snore**. Which word is **snore**? Fill in the answer circle under the word **snore**.*

## DECODING: Consonant Blends

**Objective: Recognize sound-letter relationships of consonant blends**

In administering this subtest, do not name the letters or say the sounds the letters make for the children.

Say: *Put your finger by the Sample. Look at the two letters. Next to the letters you see three pictures. I will name the three pictures for you. Choose the picture whose name begins with the sounds the letters stand for. Look at the letters in the Sample. Which picture name begins with the sounds those letters stand for? toy? trash?*

Harcourt • Reading and Language Skills Assessment

*rock? Fill in the answer circle under the picture name that begins with the sounds the letters stand for.* Pause while children mark their answers.

Then **say:** *Which picture name begins with the sounds the letters stand for?* Call on a child to provide the correct answer.

Then **say:** *Yes,* **trash** *begins with the same sounds the letters stand for in the Sample. You should have filled in the answer circle under the picture of the* **trash.** *If you did not fill in the correct answer circle, erase your mark and fill in the answer circle under the picture of the* **trash.**

Make sure that children have filled in the correct answer circle. Provide help for children who have difficulty.

Then **say:** *Now you will look at some more letters and choose the picture names that have the sounds the letters stand for. Fill in the answer circle under the pictures you choose. If you change your mind after you have marked your answer, erase your mark and fill in the answer circle under the picture you do want.*

Continue the test following the same procedures, first having children look at each pair of letters, and then having them find the picture names that begin or end with the sounds those letters stand for.

**(Beginning-sound items) Say:**

13. *Look at the letters. Which picture name begins with the sounds the letters stand for? frog? fox? rope?*
14. *Look at the letters. Which picture name begins with the sounds the letters stand for? tiger? school? store?*
15. *Look at the letters. Which picture name begins with the sounds the letters stand for? pen? press? rocket?*
16. *Look at the letters. Which picture name begins with the sounds the letters stand for? sled? swim? lion?*
17. *Look at the letters. Which picture name begins with the sounds the letters stand for? game? grass? ring?*
18. *Look at the letters. Which picture name begins with the sounds the letters stand for? sack? nest? snail?*
19. *Look at the letters. Which picture name begins with the sounds the letters stand for? razor? crab? cut?*
20. *Look at the letters. Which picture name begins with the sounds the letters stand for? soup? scoop? cage?*
21. *Look at the letters. Which picture name begins with the sounds the letters stand for? dress? river? duck?*
22. *Look at the letters. Which picture name begins with the sounds the letters stand for? pear? sun? spill?*
23. *Look at the letters. Which picture name begins with the sounds the letters stand for? mat? smell? sled?*
24. *Look at the letters. Which picture name begins with the sounds the letters stand for? skip? sun? kick?*
25. *Look at the letters. Which picture name begins with the sounds the letters stand for? web? sink? swim?*
26. *Look at the letters. Which picture name begins with the sounds the letters stand for? rope? brush? bat?*
27. *Look at the letters. Which picture name begins with the sounds the letters stand for? run? tree? tie?*

### DECODING: *Digraphs*

### Objective: Recognize sound-letter relationships of digraphs

In administering this subtest, do not say the sound the letters make or name the letters for the children.

**Say:** *Put your finger by Sample 1. Look at the two letters. Next to the letters you see three pictures. I will name the three pictures for you. Choose the picture whose name begins with the sound the letters stand for. Look at the letters in Sample 1. Which picture name begins with the sound those letters stand for? tie? shell? hat? Fill in the answer circle under the picture name that begins with the sound the letters stand for.* Pause while children mark their answers.

Then **say:** *Which picture name begins with the sound the letters stand for?* Call on a child to provide the correct answer.

Then **say:** *Yes, shell begins with the same sound the letters stand for in Sample 1. You should have filled in the answer circle under the picture of the shell. If you did not fill in the correct answer circle, erase your mark and fill in the answer circle under the picture of the shell.*

Make sure that children have filled in the correct answer circle. Provide help for children who have difficulty.

Then **say:** *Now find Sample 2 near the top of the page. Put your finger by Sample 2. Look at the two letters and the three pictures next to the letters. This time, fill in the answer circle under the picture whose name ends with the sound the letters stand for. Look at the letters in Sample 2. Which picture name ends with the sound those letters stand for? bug? clock? teeth? Fill in the answer circle under the picture name that ends with the sound the letters stand for.* Pause while children mark their answers.

Then **say:** *Which picture name ends with the same sound the letters stand for in Sample 2?* Call on a child to provide the correct answer.

Then **say:** *Yes, teeth ends with the same sound the letters stand for in Sample 2. You should have filled in the answer*

circle under the picture of the **teeth**. *If you did not fill in the correct answer circle, erase your mark and fill in the answer circle under the picture of the **teeth**.*

Make sure that children have filled in the correct answer circle. Provide help for children who have difficulty.

Then **say**: *Now you will look at some more letters and choose the picture names that have the sound the letters stand for. Fill in the answer circle under the pictures you choose. If you change your mind after you have marked your answer, erase your mark and fill in the answer circle under the picture you do want.*

Continue the test following the same procedures, first having children look at the letters, and then having them find the picture names that begin or end with the sound those letters stand for.

**(Beginning-sound items) Say:**

28. *Look at the letters. Which picture name begins with the sound the letters stand for? hose? cherries? ship?*
29. *Look at the letters. Which picture name begins with the sound the letters stand for? think? chair? butterfly?*

**Say**: *Now you will choose the picture name that **ends** with the sound the letters stand for.*

**(Ending-sound items) Say:**

30. *Look at the letters. Which picture name ends with the sound the letters stand for? bath? fire? horse?*
31. *Look at the letters. Which picture name ends with the sound the letters stand for? pail? fish? dress?*

## COMPREHENSION: *Details*

### Objective: Recognize important details in a passage

**Say**: *Put your finger by the Sample at the top of the page. Find the short story* called "Kim's Cat." We will read the story together. Follow along while I read the story aloud.

**Kim has a cat.**

**She loves her cat.**

**Each day, Kim pets the cat and plays with the cat.**

**Every night, she reads to her cat.**

Then **say:** *Find the question under the Sample story. Follow along while I read the question aloud. What does Kim do with her cat at night? pets her cat? reads to her cat? plays with her cat?* Call on a child to provide the correct answer.

Then **say:** *Yes, Kim **reads to her cat** at night. Fill in the answer circle by **reads to her cat.*** Pause while children mark their answers.

Make sure that children have filled in the correct answer circle. Provide help for children who have difficulty.

Then **say:** *Now we will read two more stories together. After we read each story, you will answer some questions about the story. Listen carefully and follow along as I read the story aloud. The first story is called "Fran's Day at School."*

**Fran walks to school with Dad.**

**She has on a new dress.**

**She sees a good friend.**

**She sees other children.**

**She sees desks to sit in and games to play.**

Then **say:** *Follow along while I read the questions aloud. Question 32 says: Who walks to school with Fran?*

**other children**

**Dad**

**a friend**

*Fill in the answer circle in front of the answer that tells who walks to school with*

Fran. Pause for children to mark their answers.

Then **say:** *Now follow along while I read the next question aloud. Question 33 says: What does Fran have that is new?*

**a dress**

**games**

**desks**

*Fill in the answer circle in front of the answer that tells what Fran has that is new.* Pause for children to mark their answers.

Then **say:** *Now we will read another story together. Listen carefully and follow along as I read the story aloud. The second story is called "A Birthday Gift."*

**Dad asked Pat what she wanted for a birthday gift.**

**She said, "I want a big red bike.**

**I will ride it to school."**

**Dad said, "I will get you the bike that you want."**

Then **say:** *Follow along while I read the questions aloud. Question 34 says: What does Pat want?*

**a game**

**a hat**

**a bike**

*Fill in the answer circle in front of the answer that tells what Pat wants.* Pause for children to mark their answers.

Then **say:** *Follow along while I read question 35 aloud. Question 35 says: What will Pat do with her gift?*

**ride it to school**

**give it to a friend**

**throw it away**

Harcourt • Reading and Language Skills Assessment

*Fill in the answer circle in front of the answer that tells what Pat will do with her gift.* Pause for children to mark their answers.

## LANGUAGE

### Objective: Recognize naming and telling parts of sentences; recognize nouns

**Say:** *Put your finger by Sample 1. You see a sentence with a word underlined in it. I will read the sentence to you. Decide whether the underlined word is the naming part of the sentence or the telling part of the sentence. The Sample 1 sentence says:*

**<u>Sam</u> hits the ball.**

*Sam is underlined. Is Sam the naming part or the telling part of the sentence? Fill in the answer circle under naming part or telling part.* Pause while children mark their answers. If you feel it is necessary, familiarize children with the terms **naming part** and **telling part**. Write the words on a chalkboard and identify them for the children.

Then **say:** *Is Sam the naming or the telling part of the sentence?* Call on a child to provide the correct answer.

Then **say:** *Yes, Sam is the naming part. You should have filled in the answer circle under naming part. If you did not fill in the correct answer circle, erase your mark completely and fill in the answer circle under naming part.*

Make sure that children have filled in the correct answer circle. Provide help for children who have difficulty.

Then **say:** *Now I will read you more sentences. Part of each sentence is underlined. Decide whether the underlined word or words are the naming or telling part of each sentence. If you change your mind after you have marked your answer, erase your mark and fill in the answer circle you*

*do want.*

Continue the test following the same procedures, having children determine whether the underlined words are the naming or telling part of each sentence. Pause after reading each question so that children can mark their answers.

Say:

36. *The sentence in this row says:* **Pam calls the cat.** *Is* **Pam** *the naming or telling part of the sentence? Mark your answer.*

37. *The sentence in this row says:* **The dog and cat do tricks.** *Is* **The dog and cat** *the naming or telling part of the sentence? Mark your answer.*

38. *The sentence in this row says:* **Ben slipped and fell.** *Is* **slipped and fell** *the naming or telling part of the sentence? Mark your answer.*

Then **say:** *Now find Sample 2 at the top of the next page. Put your finger by Sample 2. Find the sentence with some words under it. Listen while I read the sentence to you.*

**He will pick up the rock.**

*Find the words under the sentence. Fill in the answer circle by the noun that names a person, a place, an animal, or a thing.* Pause while children mark their answers.

Then **say:** *Which word names a person, a place, an animal, or a thing?* Call on a child to provide the correct answer.

Then **say:** *Yes, rock is a noun that names a thing. You should have filled in the answer circle by rock. If you did not fill in the correct answer circle, erase your mark and fill in the answer circle by rock.*

Make sure that children have filled in the correct answer circle. Provide help for children who have difficulty.

Then **say**: *Now we will read some more sentences together. Follow along while I read each sentence aloud. Then read the answer choices under each sentence and choose the word that names a person, a place, an animal, or a thing.*

Continue the test following the same procedures, reading aloud the sentences for each question. Pause after reading each sentence for children to read the answer choices independently and mark their answers.

**Say:**

**39.** *The sentence in this row says:* **The boy spins a top.** *Choose the noun that names a person, a place, an animal, or a thing.*

**40.** *The sentence in this row says:* **The fish are in a pond.** *Choose the noun that names a person, a place, an animal, or a thing.*

**41.** *The sentence in this row says:* **The doll has a red coat.** *Choose the noun that names a person, a place, an animal, or a thing.*

After all children have completed this subtest, **say**: *We have finished this activity.* Collect the assessment booklets.

Harcourt • Reading and Language Skills Assessment

# Specific Directions for Administering the *Reading and Language Skills Assessment*

....................................................................

## *Catch a Dream*/Book 1-2: POSTTEST

### *DECODING: Vowels*

Objective: Identify and isolate the medial phoneme of a spoken word (short and *R*-controlled vowels)

**Say:** *Put your finger by Sample 1. Look at the three pictures. I will tell you a sound to listen for. Then I will name the three pictures while you listen carefully. Choose the picture that has the sound I tell you. Which picture in Sample 1 has the /e/ sound? net? mug? pig? Fill in the answer circle under the picture that has the /e/ sound.* Pause while children mark their answers.

Then **say**: *Which picture has the /e/ sound?* Call on a child to provide the correct answer.

Then **say**: *Yes,* **net** *has the /e/ sound. You should have filled in the answer circle under the picture of* **net**. *If you did not fill in the correct answer circle, erase your mark completely and fill in the answer circle under the picture of* **net**.

Make sure that children have filled in the correct answer circle. Provide help for children who have difficulty.

**Say:** *Now put your finger by Sample 2. Look at the three pictures. I will tell you a sound to listen for. Choose the picture that has the sound I tell you. Which picture in Sample 2 has the /ôr/ sound? swim? sled? corn? Fill in the answer circle under the picture that has the /ôr/ sound.* Pause while children mark their answers.

Then **say**: *Which picture has the /ôr/ sound?* Call on a child to provide the correct answer.

Then **say**: *Yes,* **corn** *has the /ôr/ sound. You should have filled in the answer circle under the picture of* **corn**. *If you did not fill in the correct answer circle, erase your mark completely and fill in the answer circle under the picture of* **corn**.

Make sure that children have filled in the correct answer circle. Provide help for children who have difficulty.

Then **say**: *Now you will look at some more pictures and choose the pictures that have the sounds I tell you. Fill in the answer circle under the pictures you choose. If you change your mind after you have marked your answer, erase your mark and fill in the answer circle under the picture you do want.*

Continue the test following the same procedures, first having children listen for a specific phoneme, and then having them find the picture that has that phoneme.

**Say:**

1. *Which picture has the /e/ sound? tack? sled? frog?*
2. *Which picture has the /e/ sound? nest? light? top?*
3. *Which picture has the /u/ sound? gum? grass? gate?*
4. *Which picture has the /u/ sound? fish? flake? nut?*
5. *Which picture has the /ôr/ sound? face? storm? mice?*
6. *Which picture has the /ôr/ sound? snore? dress? bath?*

Harcourt • Reading and Language Skills Assessment

## DECODING: Vowels

### Objective: Read decodable words with short and *R*-controlled vowels

**Say:** *Put your finger on the picture of the **pet** in Sample 1. Next to the picture you see three words in a row. Find the word that names the picture. Which word is **pet**? Fill in the answer circle under the word **pet**.* Pause while children mark their answers.

Then **say:** *Which word is **pet**?* Call on a child to provide the correct answer.

Then **say:** *Yes, the first word in the row is **pet**, and it names the picture. You should have filled in the answer circle under the first word, **pet**. If you did not fill in the correct answer circle, erase your mark completely and fill in the answer circle under the first word, **pet**.*

Make sure that children have filled in the correct answer circle. Provide help for children who have difficulty.

**Say:** *Put your finger on the picture of the **stork** in Sample 2. Look at the picture and the three words in that row. Find the word that names the picture. Which word is **stork**? Fill in the answer circle under the word **stork**.* Pause while children mark their answers.

Then **say:** *Which word is **stork**?* Call on a child to provide the correct answer.

Then **say:** *Yes, the second word in the row is **stork**, and it names the picture. You should have filled in the answer circle under the second word, **stork**. If you did not fill in the correct answer circle, erase your mark completely and fill in the answer circle under the second word, **stork**.*

Make sure that children have filled in the correct answer circle. Provide help for children who have difficulty.

Then **say:** *Now you will look at some more pictures and fill in the answer circle under the word that names each picture. If you change your mind after you have marked your answer, erase your mark and fill in the answer circle under the word you do want.*

Continue the test following the same procedure, having children find the word that names each picture.

**Say:**

7. *Find the picture of a **leg**. Which word is **leg**? Fill in the answer circle under the word **leg**.*
8. *Find the picture of a **bell**. Which word is **bell**? Fill in the answer circle under the word **bell**.*
9. *Find the picture of a **duck**. Which word is **duck**? Fill in the answer circle under the word **duck**.*
10. *Find the picture of a **rug**. Which word is **rug**? Fill in the answer circle under the word **rug**.*
11. *Find the picture of a **thorn**. Which word is **thorn**? Fill in the answer circle under the word **thorn**.*
12. *Find the picture of a **fort**. Which word is **fort**? Fill in the answer circle under the word **fort**.*

## DECODING: Consonant Blends

### Objective: Recognize sound-letter relationships of consonant blends

In administering this subtest, do not name the letters or say the sounds the letters make for the children.

**Say:** *Put your finger by the Sample. Look at the two letters. Next to the letters you see three pictures. I will name the three pictures for you. Choose the picture whose name begins with the sounds the letters stand for. Look at the letters in the Sample. Which picture name begins with the sounds those letters stand for? toy? trash?*

*rock?* Fill in the answer circle under the picture name that begins with the sounds the letters stand for. Pause while children mark their answers.

Then **say**: *Which picture name begins with the sounds the letters stand for?* Call on a child to provide the correct answer.

Then **say**: *Yes,* **trash** *begins with the same sounds the letters stand for in the Sample. You should have filled in the answer circle under the picture of the* **trash**. *If you did not fill in the correct answer circle, erase your mark and fill in the answer circle under the picture of the* **trash**.

Make sure that children have filled in the correct answer circle. Provide help for children who have difficulty.

Then **say**: *Now you will look at some more letters and choose the picture names that have the sounds the letters stand for. Fill in the answer circle under the pictures you choose. If you change your mind after you have marked your answer, erase your mark and fill in the answer circle under the picture you do want.*

Continue the test following the same procedures, first having children look at each pair of letters, and then having them find the picture names that begin or end with the sounds those letters stand for.

**(Beginning-sound items) Say:**

13. *Look at the letters. Which picture name begins with the sounds the letters stand for? fruit? face? rose?*
14. *Look at the letters. Which picture name begins with the sounds the letters stand for? teeth? sun? stamp?*
15. *Look at the letters. Which picture name begins with the sounds the letters stand for? poke? pretzel? rip?*

16. *Look at the letters. Which picture name begins with the sounds the letters stand for? slip? soap? leaf?*
17. *Look at the letters. Which picture name begins with the sounds the letters stand for? goat? grapes? rocket?*
18. *Look at the letters. Which picture name begins with the sounds the letters stand for? snail? soup? nut?*
19. *Look at the letters. Which picture name begins with the sounds the letters stand for? run? crow? cat?*
20. *Look at the letters. Which picture name begins with the sounds the letters stand for? scared? sit? cap?*
21. *Look at the letters. Which picture name begins with the sounds the letters stand for? drum? rock? dove?*
22. *Look at the letters. Which picture name begins with the sounds the letters stand for? pail? sip? spoon?*
23. *Look at the letters. Which picture name begins with the sounds the letters stand for? moon? smile? sink?*
24. *Look at the letters. Which picture name begins with the sounds the letters stand for? skunk? sun? kite?*
25. *Look at the letters. Which picture name begins with the sounds the letters stand for? web? swing? saw?*
26. *Look at the letters. Which picture name begins with the sounds the letters stand for? rainbow? brick? ball?*
27. *Look at the letters. Which picture name begins with the sounds the letters stand for? rip? tape? train?*

## DECODING: *Digraphs*

### Objective: Recognize sound-letter relationships of digraphs

In administering this subtest, do not say the sound the letters make or name the letters for the children.

**Say:** *Put your finger by Sample 1. Look at the two letters. Next to the letters you see three pictures. I will name the three pictures for you. Choose the picture whose name begins with the sound the letters stand for. Look at the letters in Sample 1. Which picture name begins with the sound those letters stand for? tie? shell? hat? Fill in the answer circle under the picture name that begins with the sound the letters stand for.* Pause while children mark their answers.

Then **say:** *Which picture name begins with the sound the letters stand for?* Call on a child to provide the correct answer.

Then **say**: *Yes, **shell** begins with the same sound the letters stand for in Sample 1. You should have filled in the answer circle under the picture of the **shell**. If you did not fill in the correct answer circle, erase your mark and fill in the answer circle under the picture of the **shell**.*

Make sure that children have filled in the correct answer circle. Provide help for children who have difficulty.

Then **say:** *Now find Sample 2 near the top of the page. Put your finger by Sample 2. Look at the two letters and the three pictures next to the letters. This time, fill in the answer circle under the picture whose name **ends** with the sound the letters stand for. Look at the letters in Sample 2. Which picture name **ends** with the sound those letters stand for? bug? clock? teeth? Fill in the answer circle under the picture name that **ends** with the sound the letters stand for.* Pause while children mark their answers.

Then **say:** *Which picture name ends with same sound the letters stand for in Sample 2?* Call on a child to provide the correct answer.

Then **say**: *Yes, **teeth** ends with the same sound the letters stand for in Sample 2. You should have filled in the answer circle under the picture of the **teeth**. If you did not fill in the correct answer circle, erase your mark and fill in the answer circle under the picture of the **teeth**.*

Make sure that children have filled in the correct answer circle. Provide help for children who have difficulty.

Then **say:** *Now you will look at some more letters and choose the picture names that have the sound the letters stand for. Fill in the answer circle under the pictures you choose. If you change your mind after you have marked your answer, erase your mark and fill in the answer circle under the picture you do want.*

Continue the test following the same procedures, first having children look at the letters, and then having them find the picture names that begin or end with the sound those letters stand for.

**(Beginning-sound items) Say:**

28. *Look at the letters. Which picture name begins with the sound the letters stand for? dog? sheep? mop?*
29. *Look at the letters. Which picture name begins with the sound the letters stand for? hive? thorn? wet?*

**Say:** *Now you will choose the picture name that **ends** with the sound the letters stand for.*

**(Ending-sound items) Say:**

30. *Look at the letters. Which picture name ends with the sound the letters stand for? hen? door? moth?*
31. *Look at the letters. Which picture name ends with the sound the letters stand for? dish? pan? jar?*

## COMPREHENSION: Details

Objective: Recognize important details in a passage

**Say:** *Put your finger by the Sample at the top of the page. Find the short story called "Kim's Cat." We will read the story together. Follow along while I read the story aloud.*

> **Kim has a cat.**
>
> **She loves her cat.**
>
> **Each day, Kim pets the cat and plays with the cat.**
>
> **Every night, she reads to her cat.**

Then **say:** *Find the question under the Sample story. Follow along while I read the question aloud. What does Kim do with her cat at night? pets her cat? reads to her cat? plays with her cat? Call on a child to provide the correct answer.*

Then **say:** *Yes, Kim* **reads to her cat** *at night. Fill in the answer circle by* **reads to her cat.** *Pause while children mark their answers.*

Make sure that children have filled in the correct answer circle. Provide help for children who have difficulty.

Then **say:** *Now we will read two more stories together. After we read each story, you will answer some questions about the story. Listen carefully and follow along as I read the story aloud. The first story is called "A Hot Day."*

> **It was a very hot day.**
>
> **Carl and his friends wanted to play in the water.**
>
> **Carl's Mom came outside.**
>
> **She gave the children cold juice to drink.**
>
> **She said she would take them to the city pool.**
>
> **Carl ran to tell Dad where they were going.**

Then **say:** *Follow along while I read the questions aloud. Question 32 says:*

> **Who wants to play in the water?**
>
> **Mom**
>
> **Carl**
>
> **Dad**

*Fill in the answer circle in front of the answer that tells who wants to play in the water. Pause for children to mark their answers.*

Then **say:** *Now follow along while I read the next question aloud. Question 33 says:*

> **What do the children get to drink?**
>
> **milk**
>
> **water**
>
> **juice**

*Fill in the answer circle in front of the answer that tells what the children get to drink. Pause for children to mark their answers.*

Then **say:** *Now we will read another story together. Listen carefully and follow along as I read the story aloud. The second story is called "Picking Flowers."*

> **Sara goes out to pick flowers in her yard.**
>
> **She sees roses, lilies, pansies, and buttercups.**
>
> **Sara picks four red roses to give to Grandma.**
>
> **Roses are Grandma's favorite flower.**

Then **say:** *Follow along while I read the questions aloud. Question 34 says:*

> **Which flower does Sara pick?**
>
> **lilies**
>
> **pansies**
>
> **roses**

*Fill in the answer circle in front of the answer that tells which flower Sara picks.*

Harcourt • Reading and Language Skills Assessment

Pause for children to mark their answers.

Then **say:** *Follow along while I read question 35 aloud. Question 35 says:*

**How many flowers will Sara give Grandma?**

**one**

**three**

**four**

*Fill in the answer circle in front of the answer that tells how many flowers Sara will give Grandma.* Pause for children to mark their answers.

### LANGUAGE

**Objective: Recognize naming and telling parts of sentences; recognize nouns**

**Say:** *Put your finger by Sample 1. You see a sentence with a word underlined in it. I will read the sentence to you. Decide whether the underlined word is the naming part of the sentence or the telling part of the sentence. The Sample 1 sentence says:*

**<u>Sam</u> hits the ball.**

*Sam is underlined. Is **Sam** the naming part or the telling part of the sentence? Fill in the answer circle under naming part or telling part.* Pause while children mark their answers. If you feel it is necessary, familiarize children with the terms **naming part** and **telling part**. Write the words on a chalkboard and identify them for the children.

Then **say:** *Is **Sam** the naming or the telling part of the sentence?* Call on a child to provide the correct answer.

Then **say:** *Yes, **Sam** is the naming part. You should have filled in the answer circle under **naming part**. If you did not fill in the correct answer circle, erase your mark completely and fill in the answer circle under **naming part**.*

Make sure that children have filled in the correct answer circle. Provide help for children who have difficulty.

Then **say:** *Now I will read you more sentences. Part of each sentence is underlined. Decide whether the underlined word or words are the naming or telling part of each sentence. If you change your mind after you have marked your answer, erase your mark and fill in the answer circle you do want.*

Continue the test following the same procedures, having children determine whether the underlined words are the naming or telling part of each sentence. Pause after reading each question so that children can mark their answers.

**Say:**

**36.** *The sentence in this row says: **That pot is hot**. Is **That pot** the naming or telling part of the sentence? Mark your answer.*

**37.** *The sentence in this row says: **My friend and I play ball**. Is **My friend and I** the naming or telling part of the sentence? Mark your answer.*

**38.** *The sentence in this row says: **Jan ran and jumped**. Is **ran and jumped** the naming or telling part of the sentence? Mark your answer.*

Then **say:** *Now find Sample 2 at the top of the next page. Put your finger by Sample 2. Find the sentence with some words under it. Listen while I read the sentence to you.*

**He will pick up the rock.**

*Find the words under the sentence. Fill in the answer circle by the noun that names a person, a place, an animal, or a thing.* Pause while children mark their answers.

Then **say:** *Which word names a person, a place, an animal, or a thing?*

Harcourt • Reading and Language Skills Assessment

Call on a child to provide the correct answer.

Then **say:** *Yes, rock is a noun that names a thing. You should have filled in the answer circle by rock. If you did not fill in the correct answer circle, erase your mark and fill in the answer circle by rock.*

Make sure that children have filled in the correct answer circle. Provide help for children who have difficulty.

Then **say:** *Now we will read some more sentences together. Follow along while I read each sentence aloud. Then read the answer choices under each sentence and choose the word that names a person, a place, an animal, or a thing.*

Continue the test following the same procedures, reading aloud the sentences for each question. Pause after reading each sentence for children to read the answer choices independently and mark their answers.

**Say:**

39. *The sentence in this row says:* **The girl has a penny.** *Choose the noun that names a person, a place, an animal, or a thing.*

40. *The sentence in this row says:* **The pigs are in a pen.** *Choose the noun that names a person, a place, an animal, or a thing.*

41. *The sentence in this row says:* **The truck has a loud horn.** *Choose the noun that names a person, a place, an animal, or a thing.*

After all children have completed this subtest, **say:** *We have finished this activity.* Collect the assessment booklets.

Harcourt • Reading and Language Skills Assessment

# Specific Directions for Administering the *Reading and Language Skills Assessment*

● ● ● ● ● ● ● ● ● ● ● ● ● ● ● ● ● ● ● ● ● ● ● ● ● ● ● ● ● ● ● ● ● ● ● ● ● ● ● ● ● ● ● ● ● ● ● ● ● ● ● ● ●

## *Here and There*/Book 1-3: PRETEST

### DECODING: *Vowels*

**Objective: Identify and isolate the medial phoneme of a spoken word (long and *R*-controlled vowels)**

**Say:** *Put your finger by Sample 1. Look at the three pictures. I will tell you a sound to listen for. Then I will name the three pictures while you listen carefully. Choose the picture that has the sound I tell you. Which picture has the /ō/ sound? swim? sled? coat? Fill in the answer circle under the picture that has the /ō/ sound.* Pause while children mark their answers.

Then **say:** *Which picture has the /ō/ sound?* Call on a child to provide the correct answer.

Then **say:** *Yes, **coat** has the /ō/ sound. You should have filled in the answer circle under the picture of **coat**. If you did not fill in the correct answer circle, erase your mark completely and fill in the answer circle under the picture of **coat**.*

Make sure that children have filled in the correct answer circle. Provide help for children who have difficulty.

**Say:** *Now put your finger by Sample 2. Look at the three pictures. I will tell you a sound to listen for. Choose the picture that has the sound I tell you. Which picture in Sample 2 has the /är/ sound? gum? park? snake? Fill in the answer circle under the picture that has the /är/ sound.* Pause while children mark their answers.

Then **say:** *Which picture has the /är/ sound?* Call on a child to provide the correct answer.

Then **say:** *Yes, **park** has the /är/ sound. You should have filled in the answer circle under the picture of **park**. If you did not fill in the correct answer circle, erase your mark completely and fill in the answer circle under the picture of **park**.*

Make sure that children have filled in the correct answer circle. Provide help for children who have difficulty.

Then **say:** *Now you will look at some more pictures and choose the pictures that have the sounds I tell you. Fill in the answer circle under the pictures you choose. If you change your mind after you have marked your answer, erase your mark and fill in the answer circle under the picture you do want.*

Continue the test following the same procedures, first having children listen for a specific phoneme, and then having them find the picture that has that phoneme.

**Say:**

1. *Which picture has the /ō/ sound? boat? price? ship?*
2. *Which picture has the /ō/ sound? glue? crow? tape?*
3. *Which picture has the /är/ sound? bus? jar? sheep?*
4. *Which picture has the /är/ sound? chick? feet? cart?*
5. *Which picture has the /ûr/ sound? skirt? tray? cone?*
6. *Which picture has the /ûr/ sound? leaf? flag? purse?*

## DECODING: Vowels

**Objective: Read decodable words with long vowels and *R*-controlled vowels**

**Say:** *Put your finger by Sample 1. Look at the picture. Next to the picture you see three words in a row. Find the word that names the picture. Put your finger on the picture of the goat in Sample 1. Which word is **goat**? Fill in the answer circle under the word **goat**.* Pause while children mark their answers.

Then **say:** *Which word is **goat**?* Call on a child to provide the correct answer.

Then **say:** *Yes, the last word in the row is **goat**, and it names the picture. You should have filled in the answer circle under the last word, **goat**. If you did not fill in the correct answer circle, erase your mark completely and fill in the answer circle under the last word, **goat**.*

Make sure that children have filled in the correct answer circle. Provide help for children who have difficulty.

**Say:** *Put your finger on the picture of the jug in Sample 2. Look at the picture and the three words in that row. Find the word that names the picture. Which word is **park**? Fill in the answer circle under the word **park**.* Pause while children mark their answers.

Then **say:** *Which word is **park**?* Call on a child to provide the correct answer.

Then **say:** *Yes, the second word in the row is **park**, and it names the picture. You should have filled in the answer circle under the second word, **park**. If you did not fill in the correct answer circle, erase your mark completely and fill in the answer circle under the second word, **park**.*

Make sure that children have filled in the correct answer circle. Provide help for children who have difficulty.

Then **say:** *Now you will look at some more pictures and fill in the answer circle under the word that names each picture. If you change your mind after you have marked your answer, erase your mark and fill in the answer circle under the word you do want.*

Continue the test following the same procedure, having children find the word that names each picture.

**Say:**

7. *Find the picture of a **coat**. Which word is **coat**? Fill in the answer circle under the word **coat**.*

8. *Find the picture of **crow**. Which word is **crow**? Fill in the answer circle under the word **crow**.*

9. *Find the picture of a **barn**. Which word is **barn**? Fill in the answer circle under the word **barn**.*

10. *Find the picture of **card**. Which word is **card**? Fill in the answer circle under the word **card**.*

11. *Find the picture of a **bird**. Which word is **bird**? Fill in the answer circle under the word **bird**.*

12. *Find the picture of **third**. Which word is **third**? Fill in the answer circle under the word **third**.*

## DECODING: Initial Blends

**Objective: Recognize sound-letter relationships of initial consonant blends**

In administering this subtest, do not name the letters or say the sounds the letters make for the children.

**Say:** *Put your finger by the Sample. Look at the two letters. Next to the letters you see three pictures. I will name the three pictures for you. Choose the picture whose name begins with the sounds the letters stand for. Look at the letters in the Sample. Which picture name begins with the* sounds those letters stand for? pan? laugh? plum? Fill in the answer circle under the picture name that begins with the sounds the letters stand for. Pause while children mark their answers.

Then **say**: *Which picture name begins with the sounds the letters stand for?* Call on a child to provide the correct answer.

Then **say**: *Yes, **plum** begins with the same sounds the letters stand for in the Sample. You should have filled in the answer circle under the picture of the **plum**. If you did not fill in the correct answer circle, erase your mark and fill in the answer circle under the picture of the **plum**.*

Make sure that children have filled in the correct answer circle. Provide help for children who have difficulty.

Then **say**: *Now you will look at some more letters and choose the picture names that have the sounds the letters stand for. Fill in the answer circle under the pictures you choose. If you change your mind after you have marked your answer, erase your mark and fill in the answer circle under the picture you do want.*

Continue the test following the same procedures, first having children look at each pair of letters, and then having them find the picture names that begin with the sounds of those letters.

**(Beginning-sound items) Say:**

13. *Look at the letters. Which picture name begins with the sounds the letters stand for? blow? lamp? book?*
14. *Look at the letters. Which picture name begins with the sounds the letters stand for? lip? class? cone?*
15. *Look at the letters. Which picture name begins with the sounds the letters stand for? flag? fish? leaf?*

16. *Look at the letters. Which picture name begins with the sounds the letters stand for? light? grab? glass?*
17. *Look at the letters. Which picture name begins with the sounds the letters stand for? pear? plant? lid?*
18. *Look at the letters. Which picture name begins with the sounds the letters stand for? lock? slip? scared?*

### DECODING: Digraphs

## Objective: Recognize sound-letter relationships of digraphs

In administering this subtest, do not name the letters for the children or say the sound the letters.

**Say**: *Put your finger by Sample 1. Look at the two letters. Next to the letters you see three pictures. I will name the three pictures for you. Choose the picture whose name begins with the sound the letters stand for. Look at the letters in Sample 1. Which picture name begins with the sound those letters stand for? quilt? ship? cap? Fill in the answer circle under the picture name that begins with the sound the letters stand for. Pause while children mark their answers.*

Then **say**: *Which picture name begins with the sound the letters stand for?* Call on a child to provide the correct answer.

Then **say**: *Yes, **quilt** begins with the same sound the letters stand for in Sample 1. You should have filled in the answer circle under the picture of the **quilt**. If you did not fill in the correct answer circle, erase your mark and fill in the answer circle under the picture of the **quilt**.*

Make sure that children have filled in the correct answer circle. Provide help for children who have difficulty.

Then **say**: *Now find Sample 2 near the top of the page. Put your finger by*

Harcourt • Reading and Language Skills Assessment

*Sample 2. Look at the two letters and the three pictures next to the letters. Fill in the answer circle under the picture whose name* **ends** *with the sound the letters stand for. Look at the letters in sample 2. Which picture name* **ends** *with the sound those letters stand for? dish? shell? branch? Fill in the answer circle under the picture name that ends with the sound the letters stand for. Pause while children mark their answers.*

Then **say**: *Which picture name ends with the same sound the letters stand for in Sample 2?* Call on a child to provide the correct answer.

Then **say**: *Yes,* **branch** *ends with the same sound the letters stand for in Sample 2. You should have filled in the answer circle under the picture of the* **branch**. *If you did not fill in the correct answer circle, erase your mark and fill in the answer circle under the picture of the* **branch**.

Make sure that children have filled in the correct answer circle. Provide help for children who have difficulty.

Then **say**: *Now you will look at some more letters and choose the picture names that have the sound the letters stand for. Fill in the answer circle under the pictures you choose. If you change your mind after you have marked your answer, erase your mark and fill in the answer circle under the picture you do want.*

Continue the test following the same procedures, first having children look at the letters, and then having them find the picture names that begin or end with the sound the letters stand for.

**(Beginning-sound items) Say:**

19. *Look at the letters. Which picture name begins with the sound the letters stand for? shed? chick? crow?*

20. *Look at the letters. Which picture name begins with the sound the letters stand for? bag? dress? quack?*

21. *Look at the letters. Which picture name begins with the sound the letters stand for? whistle? weeds? house?*

22. *Look at the letters. Which picture name begins with the sound the letters stand for? queen? belt? gum?*

23. *Look at the letters. Which picture name begins with the sound the letters stand for? web? wheat? hoe?*

**Say**: *The last question is a little different. On this question, you will choose the picture name that* **ends** *with the sound the letters stand for.*

**(Ending-sound item) Say:**

24. *Look at the letters. Which picture name ends with the sound the letters stand for? kick? lunch? push?*

## DECODING: *Inflections*

**Objective: Recognize inflectional endings with no spelling changes**

In reading aloud the sentences on this subtest, you may use the word *blank* or simply pause where the tested word is missing.

**Say**: *Look at the Sample at the top of the page. You see a sentence with a blank where a word is missing. There are three words under the sentence. I will read the sentence to you. You will read the words under the sentence. Then you will choose the word that best completes the sentence. The Sample sentence says:*

> *He _____ the ball.*

*Now read the three words under the sentence. Which word makes sense in the sentence? Fill in the answer circle under the word that best completes the sentence.* Pause while children mark their answers.

Harcourt • Reading and Language Skills Assessment

Then **say:** *Which word best completes the sentence?* Call on a child to provide the correct answer.

Then **say:** *Yes, the word **kicked** best fits in the blank to complete the sentence. **He kicked the ball.** You should have filled in the answer circle under the word **kicked**. If you did not fill in the correct answer circle, erase your mark and fill in the answer circle under the word **kicked.***

Then **say:** *Now I will read you some more sentences that have a word missing. Read the words under the sentences. Then choose the word that best completes each sentence.*

Continue the test following the same procedures, first reading each sentence aloud to the children, then pausing while they choose the word that completes each sentence.

**Say:**

25. *The sentence in this row says: **The boat is _____.** Find the word that best completes the sentence.*
26. *The sentence in this row says: **We _____ for the lost book.** Find the word that best completes the sentence.*
27. *The sentence in this row says: **Dad is _____ Sam.** Find the word that best completes the sentence.*
28. *The sentence in this row says: **Fran _____ her lunch.** Find the word that best completes the sentence.*

### COMPREHENSION: *Setting and Character*

**Objective: Identify and describe the elements of setting and character in a story**

**Say:** *Put your finger by the Sample at the top of the page. Find the short story called "Ben Plays Ball." We will read the story together. Follow along while I read the story aloud.*

*One day, Ben went to Sam's house.*

*Sam got a bat, and Ben got a ball.*

*They played ball and had fun.*

Then **say:** *Find the question under the Sample story: Follow along while I read the question aloud. **Where did this story take place? in a barn? at a store? at Sam's house?** Call on a child to provide the correct answer.*

Then **say:** *Yes, the story takes place **at Sam's house.** Fill in the answer circle by **at Sam's house.** Pause while children mark their answers.*

Make sure that children have filled in the correct answer circle. Provide help for children who have difficulty.

Then **say:** *Now I want you to read two more stories and answer the questions by yourself. Keep working until you come to the word "Stop." When you come to the word Stop, put your pencils down. Sit quietly until everyone is finished.*

### LANGUAGE

**Objective: Recognize nouns and proper nouns**

**Say:** *Put your finger by Sample 1. Find the sentence with some words under it. Listen while I read the sentence to you.*

**She will throw the ball.**

*Find the words under the sentence. Fill in the answer circle by the noun that names a person, a place, an animal, or a thing. Pause while children mark their answers.*

Then **say:** *Which word names a person, a place, an animal, or a thing?* Call on a child to provide the correct answer.

Then **say**: *Yes, **ball** is a noun that names a thing. You should have filled in the answer circle by **ball**. If you did not fill in the correct answer circle, erase your mark and fill in the answer circle by **ball**.*

Make sure that children have filled in the correct answer circle. Provide help for children who have difficulty.

Then **say**: *Now we will read some more sentences together. Follow along while I read each sentence aloud. Then read the answer choices under each sentence and choose the word that names a person, a place, an animal, or a thing.*

Continue the test following the same procedures, reading aloud the sentences for each question. Pause after reading each sentence for children to read the answer choices independently and mark their answers.

**Say:**

35. *The sentence in this row says: **The pig is in a pen**. Choose the noun that names a person, a place, an animal, or a thing.*

36. *The sentence in this row says: **I see a pretty horse**. Choose the noun that names a person, a place, an animal, or a thing.*

   **Say:** *Now put your finger by Sample 2. Find the sentence with some words under it. Listen while I read the sentence to you.*

   ***My teacher is Mr. Simms.***

   *Find the words under the sentence. Fill in the answer circle by the noun that names a special person or a special place. Pause while children mark their answers.*

   Then **say**: *Which noun names a spe-*

*cial person or a special place?* Call on a child to provide the correct answer.

Then **say**: *Yes, **Mr. Simms** is a noun that names a special person. You should have filled in the answer circle by **Mr. Simms**. If you did not fill in the correct answer circle, erase your mark and fill in the answer circle by **Mr. Simms**.*

Make sure that children have filled in the correct answer circle. Provide help for children who have difficulty.

Then **say**: *Now we will read some more sentences together. Follow along while I read each sentence aloud. Then read the answer choices under each sentence and choose the word that names a special person or a special place.*

Continue the test following the same procedures, reading aloud the sentences for each question. Pause after reading each sentence for children to read the answer choices independently and mark their answers.

37. *The sentence in this row says: **Mr. Smith is my friend**. Choose the noun that names a special person or a special place.*

38. *The sentence in this row says: **We live on Hill Street**. Choose the noun that names a special person or a special place.*

39. *The sentence in this row says: **Soon Uncle Ned will be here**. Choose the noun that names a special person or a special place.*

40. *The sentence in this row says: **We are going to Sun Park**. Choose the noun that names a special person or a special place.*

After all children have completed this subtest, **say**: *We have finished this activity.* Collect the assessment booklets.

Harcourt • Reading and Language Skills Assessment

# Specific Directions for Administering the *Reading and Language Skills Assessment*

...............................................................

## Here and There/Book 1-3: POSTTEST

### DECODING: Vowels

**Objective: Identify and isolate the medial phoneme of a spoken word (long and *R*-controlled vowels)**

**Say:** *Put your finger by Sample 1. Look at the three pictures. I will tell you a sound to listen for. Then I will name the three pictures while you listen carefully. Choose the picture that has the sound I tell you. Which picture has the /ō/ sound? swim? sled? coat? Fill in the answer circle under the picture that has the /ō/ sound.* Pause while children mark their answers.

Then **say:** *Which picture has the /ō/ sound?* Call on a child to provide the correct answer.

Then **say:** *Yes, **coat** has the /ō/ sound. You should have filled in the answer circle under the picture of **coat**. If you did not fill in the correct answer circle, erase your mark completely and fill in the answer circle under the picture of **coat**.*

Make sure that children have filled in the correct answer circle. Provide help for children who have difficulty.

**Say:** *Now put your finger by Sample 2. Look at the three pictures. I will tell you a sound to listen for. Choose the picture that has the sound I tell you. Which picture in Sample 2 has the /är/ sound? gum? park? snake? Fill in the answer circle under the picture that has the /är/ sound.* Pause while children mark their answers.

Then **say:** *Which picture has the /är/ sound?* Call on a child to provide the correct answer.

Then **say:** *Yes, **park** has the /är/ sound. You should have filled in the answer circle under the picture of **park**. If you did not fill in the correct answer circle, erase your mark completely and fill in the answer circle under the picture of **park**.*

Make sure that children have filled in the correct answer circle. Provide help for children who have difficulty.

Then **say:** *Now you will look at some more pictures and choose the pictures that have the sounds I tell you. Fill in the answer circle under the pictures you choose. If you change your mind after you have marked your answer, erase your mark and fill in the answer circle under the picture you do want.*

Continue the test following the same procedures, first having children listen for a specific phoneme, and then having them find the picture that has that phoneme.

**Say:**

1. *Which picture has the /ō/ sound? dress? goat? nut?*
2. *Which picture has the /ō/ sound? chest? dish? snow?*
3. *Which picture has the /är/ sound? harp? jet? bat?*
4. *Which picture has the /är/ sound? pig? star? map?*
5. *Which picture has the /ûr/ sound? bike? girl? fan?*
6. *Which picture has the /ûr/ sound? shirt? bell? mitt?*

**DECODING: Vowels**

**Objective: Read decodable words with long vowels and *R*-controlled vowels**

**Say:** *Put your finger by Sample 1. Look at the picture. Next to the picture you see three words in a row. Find the word that names the picture. Put your finger on the picture of the goat in Sample 1. Which word is **goat**? Fill in the answer circle under the word **goat**.* Pause while children mark their answers.

Then **say:** *Which word is **goat**?* Call on a child to provide the correct answer.

Then **say:** *Yes, the last word in the row is **goat**, and it names the picture. You should have filled in the answer circle under the last word, **goat**. If you did not fill in the correct answer circle, erase your mark completely and fill in the answer circle under the last word, **goat**.*

Make sure that children have filled in the correct answer circle. Provide help for children who have difficulty.

**Say:** *Put your finger on the picture of the park in Sample 2. Look at the picture and the three words in that row. Find the word that names the picture. Which word is **park**? Fill in the answer circle under the word **park**.* Pause while children mark their answers.

Then **say:** *Which word is **park**?* Call on a child to provide the correct answer.

Then **say:** *Yes, the second word in the row is **park**, and it names the picture. You should have filled in the answer circle under the second word, **park**. If you did not fill in the correct answer circle, erase your mark completely and fill in the answer circle under the second word, **park**.*

Make sure that children have filled in the correct answer circle. Provide help for children who have difficulty.

Then **say:** *Now you will look at some more pictures and fill in the answer circle under the word that names each picture. If you change your mind after you have marked your answer, erase your mark and fill in the answer circle under the word you do want.*

Continue the test following the same procedure, having children find the word that names each picture.

**Say:**

7. *Find the picture of a **road**. Which word is **road**? Fill in the answer circle under the word **road**.*
8. *Find the picture of **throw**. Which word is **throw**? Fill in the answer circle under the word **throw**.*
9. *Find the picture of a **harp**. Which word is **harp**? Fill in the answer circle under the word **harp**.*
10. *Find the picture of **cart**. Which word is **cart**? Fill in the answer circle under the word **cart**.*
11. *Find the picture of a **first**. Which word is **first**? Fill in the answer circle under the word **first**.*
12. *Find the picture of **girl**. Which word is **girl**? Fill in the answer circle under the word **girl**.*

**DECODING: Initial Blends**

**Objective: Recognize sound-letter relationships of initial consonant blends**

In administering this subtest, do not name the letters or say the sounds the letters make for the children.

**Say:** *Put your finger by the Sample. Look at the two letters. Next to the letters you see three pictures. I will name the three pictures for you. Choose the picture whose name begins with the sounds the letters stand for. Look at the letters in the Sample. Which picture name begins with the* sounds those letters stand for? pan? laugh? plum? Fill in the answer circle under the picture name that begins with the sounds the letters stand for. Pause while children mark their answers.

Then **say**: *Which picture name begins with the sounds the letters stand for? Call on a child to provide the correct answer.*

Then **say**: *Yes, **plum** begins with the same sounds the letters stand for in the Sample. You should have filled in the answer circle under the picture of the **plum**. If you did not fill in the correct answer circle, erase your mark and fill in the answer circle under the picture of the **plum**.*

Make sure that children have filled in the correct answer circle. Provide help for children who have difficulty.

Then **say**: *Now you will look at some more letters and choose the picture names that have the sounds the letters stand for. Fill in the answer circle under the pictures you choose. If you change your mind after you have marked your answer, erase your mark and fill in the answer circle under the picture you do want.*

Continue the test following the same procedures, first having children look at each pair of letters, and then having them find the picture names that begin with the sounds of those letters.

**(Beginning-sound items) Say:**

13. *Look at the letters. Which picture name begins with the sounds the letters stand for? ball? block? leaf?*
14. *Look at the letters. Which picture name begins with the sounds the letters stand for? clap? lion? cake?*
15. *Look at the letters. Which picture name begins with the sounds the letters stand for? light? fan? fly?*

16. *Look at the letters. Which picture name begins with the sounds the letters stand for? glue? gate? leg?*
17. *Look at the letters. Which picture name begins with the sounds the letters stand for? pin? lip? plant?*
18. *Look at the letters. Which picture name begins with the sounds the letters stand for? sit? sled? lock?*

### DECODING: *Digraphs*

## Objective: Recognize sound-letter relationships of digraphs

In administering this subtest, do not name the letters for the children or say the sound the letters.

**Say**: *Put your finger by Sample 1. Look at the two letters. Next to the letters you see three pictures. I will name the three pictures for you. Choose the picture whose name begins with the sound the letters stand for. Look at the letters in Sample 1. Which picture name begins with the sound those letters stand for? quilt? ship? cap? Fill in the answer circle under the picture name that begins with the sound the letters stand for. Pause while children mark their answers.*

Then **say**: *Which picture name begins with the sound the letters stand for? Call on a child to provide the correct answer.*

Then **say**: *Yes, **quilt** begins with the same sound the letters stand for in Sample 1. You should have filled in the answer circle under the picture of the **quilt**. If you did not fill in the correct answer circle, erase your mark and fill in the answer circle under the picture of the **quilt**.*

Make sure that children have filled in the correct answer circle. Provide help for children who have difficulty.

Then **say**: *Now find Sample 2 near the top of the page. Put your finger by*

Sample 2. Look at the two letters and the three pictures next to the letters. Fill in the answer circle under the picture whose name **ends** with the sound the letters stand for. Look at the letters in Sample 2. Which picture name **ends** with the sound those letters stand for? dish? shell? branch? Fill in the answer circle under the picture name that ends with the sound the letters stand for. Pause while children mark their answers.

Then **say**: Which picture name ends with the same sound the letters stand for in Sample 2? Call on a child to provide the correct answer.

Then **say**: Yes, **branch** ends with the same sound the letters stand for in Sample 2. You should have filled in the answer circle under the picture of the **branch**. If you did not fill in the correct answer circle, erase your mark and fill in the answer circle under the picture of the **branch**.

Make sure that children have filled in the correct answer circle. Provide help for children who have difficulty.

Then **say**: Now you will look at some more letters and choose the picture names that have the sound the letters stand for. Fill in the answer circle under the pictures you choose. If you change your mind after you have marked your answer, erase your mark and fill in the answer circle under the picture you do want.

Continue the test following the same procedures, first having children look at the letters, and then having them find the picture names that begin or end with the sound the letters stand for.

(Beginning-sound items) Say:

19. Look at the letters. Which picture name begins with the sound the letters stand for? shell? chest? crow?

20. Look at the letters. Which picture name begins with the sound the letters stand for? frog? snail? quarter?

21. Look at the letters. Which picture name begins with the sound the letters stand for? whip? wig? hen?

22. Look at the letters. Which picture name begins with the sound the letters stand for? question? hive? sheep?

23. Look at the letters. Which picture name begins with the sound the letters stand for? wet? wheel? hut?

**Say**: The last question is a little different. On this question, you will choose the picture name that **ends** with the sound the letters stand for.

(Ending-sound item) Say:

24. Look at the letters. Which picture name ends with the sound the letters stand for? lock? catch? fish?

## DECODING: Inflections

### Objective: Recognize inflectional endings with no spelling changes

In reading aloud the sentences on this subtest, you may use the word *blank* or simply pause where the tested word is missing.

**Say**: Look at the Sample at the top of the page. You see a sentence with a blank where a word is missing. There are three words under the sentence. I will read the sentence to you. You will read the words under the sentence. Then you will choose the word that best completes the sentence. The Sample sentence says:

**He _____ the ball.**

Now read the three words under the sentence. Which word makes sense in the sentence? Fill in the answer circle under the word that best completes the sentence. Pause while children mark their answers.

Harcourt • Reading and Language Skills Assessment

Then **say**: *Which word best completes the sentence?* Call on a child to provide the correct answer.

Then **say**: *Yes, the word **kicked** best fits in the blank to complete the sentence.* **He kicked the ball.** *You should have filled in the answer circle under the word **kicked**. If you did not fill in the correct answer circle, erase your mark and fill in the answer circle under the word **kicked**.*

Then **say**: *Now I will read you some more sentences that have a word missing. Read the words under the sentences. Then choose the word that best completes each sentence.*

Continue the test following the same procedures, first reading each sentence aloud to the children, then pausing while they choose the word that completes each sentence.

**Say:**

25. *The sentence in this row says:* **Jeff is _____.** *Find the word that best completes the sentence.*
26. *The sentence in this row says:* **They _____ for the lost cat.** *Find the word that best completes the sentence.*
27. *The sentence in this row says:* **The dog is _____ at me.** *Find the word that best completes the sentence.*
28. *The sentence in this row says:* **She _____ the egg.** *Find the word that best completes the sentence.*

## COMPREHENSION: Setting and Character

**Objective: Identify and describe the elements of setting and character in a story**

**Say:** *Put your finger by the Sample at the top of the page. Find the short story called "Ben Plays Ball." We will read the story together. Follow along while I read the story aloud.*

*One day, Ben went to Sam's house.*

*Sam got a bat, and Ben got a ball.*

*They played ball and had fun.*

Then **say**: *Find the question under the Sample story: Follow along while I read the question aloud.* **Where did this story take place? in a barn? at a store? at Sam's house?** *Call on a child to provide the correct answer.*

Then **say**: *Yes, the story takes place **at Sam's house.** Fill in the answer circle by **at Sam's house.** Pause while children mark their answers.*

Make sure that children have filled in the correct answer circle. Provide help for children who have difficulty.

Then **say**: *Now I want you to read two more stories and answer the questions by yourself. Keep working until you come to the word "Stop." When you come to the word Stop, put your pencils down. Sit quietly until everyone is finished.*

## LANGUAGE

### Objective: Recognize nouns and proper nouns

**Say:** *Put your finger by Sample 1. Find the sentence with some words under it. Listen while I read the sentence to you.*

**She will throw the ball.**

*Find the words under the sentence. Fill in the answer circle by the noun that names a person, a place, an animal, or a thing. Pause while children mark their answers.*

Then **say**: *Which word names a person, a place, an animal, or a thing? Call on a child to provide the correct answer.*

Then **say**: *Yes, **ball** is a noun that names a thing. You should have filled in the answer circle by **ball**. If you did not fill*

Harcourt • Reading and Language Skills Assessment

*in the correct answer circle, erase your mark and fill in the answer circle by* **ball**.

Make sure that children have filled in the correct answer circle. Provide help for children who have difficulty.

Then **say**: *Now we will read some more sentences together. Follow along while I read each sentence aloud. Then read the answer choices under each sentence and choose the word that names a person, a place, an animal, or a thing.*

Continue the test following the same procedures, reading aloud the sentences for each question. Pause after reading each sentence for children to read the answer choices independently and mark their answers.

**Say:**

**35.** *The sentence in this row says:* **The fish splashes in the pond**. *Choose the noun that names a person, a place, an animal, or a thing.*

**36.** *The sentence in this row says:* **We saw some chickens**. *Choose the noun that names a person, a place, an animal, or a thing.*

**Say**: *Now put your finger by Sample 2. Find the sentence with some words under it. Listen while I read the sentence to you.*

**My teacher is Mr. Simms.**

*Find the words under the sentence. Fill in the answer circle by the noun that names a special person or a special place. Pause while children mark their answers.*

Then **say**: *Which noun names a special person or a special place?* Call on a child to provide the correct answer.

Then **say**: *Yes,* **Mr. Simms** *is a noun that names a special person. You should have filled in the answer circle by* **Mr. Simms.** *If you did not fill in the correct answer circle, erase your mark and fill in the answer circle by* **Mr. Simms.**

Make sure that children have filled in the correct answer circle. Provide help for children who have difficulty.

Then **say**: *Now we will read some more sentences together. Follow along while I read each sentence aloud. Then read the answer choices under each sentence and choose the word that names a special person or a special place.*

Continue the test following the same procedures, reading aloud the sentences for each question. Pause after reading each sentence for children to read the answer choices independently and mark their answers.

**37.** *The sentence in this row says:* **I see Dr. Mills when I am sick**. *Choose the noun that names a special person or a special place.*

**38.** *The sentence in this row says:* **My house is on Park Street**. *Choose the noun that names a special person or a special place.*

**39.** *The sentence in this row says:* **Soon Mrs. Conn will be here**. *Choose the noun that names a special person or a special place.*

**40.** *The sentence in this row says:* **We had fun at Pebble Pond**. *Choose the noun that names a special person or a special place.*

After all children have completed this subtest, **say**: *We have finished this activity.* Collect the assessment booklets.

Harcourt • Reading and Language Skills Assessment

# Specific Directions for Administering the *Reading and Language Skills Assessment*

∙∙∙∙∙∙∙∙∙∙∙∙∙∙∙∙∙∙∙∙∙∙∙∙∙∙∙∙∙∙∙∙∙∙∙∙∙∙∙∙∙∙∙∙∙∙∙∙∙∙∙∙∙

## *Time Together*/Book 1-4
### PRETEST

### *DECODING: Vowels*

**Objective: Read decodable words with long vowels**

**Say:** *Put your finger on the picture of the pole in the Sample. Next to the picture you see three words in that row. Find the word that names the picture. Which word is* **pole**? *Fill in the answer circle under the word* **pole**. Pause while children mark their answers.

Then **say:** *Which word is* **pole**? Call on a child to provide the correct answer.

Then **say:** *Yes, the second word in the row is* **pole**, *and it names the picture. You should have filled in the answer circle under the second word,* **pole**. *If you did not fill in the correct answer circle, erase your mark completely and fill in the answer circle under the second word,* **pole**.

Make sure that children have filled in the correct answer circle. Provide help for children who have difficulty.

Then **say:** *Now you will look at some more pictures and fill in the answer circle under the word that names each picture. If you change your mind after you have marked your answer, erase your mark and fill in the answer circle under the word you do want.*

Continue the test following the same procedures, having children find the word that names each picture.

**Say:**

1. *Find the picture of the* **sheep**. *Which word is* **sheep**? *Fill in the answer circle under the word* **sheep**.

2. *Find the picture of* **read**. *Which word is* **read**? *Fill in the answer circle under the word* **read**.

3. *Find the picture of a* **spike**. *Which word is* **spike**? *Fill in the answer circle under the word* **spike**.

4. *Find the picture of a* **bike**. *Which word is* **bike**? *Fill in the answer circle under the word* **bike**.

5. *Find the picture of a* **skate**. *Which word is* **skate**? *Fill in the answer circle under the word* **skate**.

6. *Find the picture of a* **lake**. *Which word is* **lake**? *Fill in the answer circle under the word* **lake**.

7. *Find the picture of a* **dome**. *Which word is* **dome**? *Fill in the answer circle under the word dome*

8. *Find the picture of a* **mole**. *Which word is* **mole**? *Fill in the answer circle under the word* **mole**.

### *DECODING: Word Structure*

**Objective: Recognize contractions**

**Say:** *Look at the Sample at the top of the page. Find the sentence with a word underlined. We will read the sentence together. Follow along while I read the sentence aloud.*

**<u>I'll</u> read the book to you.**

Then **say:** *Look at the underlined word,* **I'll**. *Read the answer choices under the sentence. Which words under the sentence mean the same as* **I'll**? Call on a child to provide the correct answer.

Then **say**: *Yes, **I will** means the same as **I'll**. Fill in the answer circle under the words **I will**.* Make sure that children have filled in the correct answer circle. Provide help for children who have difficulty.

Then **say**: *Now I want you to read some more sentences by yourself. First, read each sentence with an underlined word. Then read the words under the sentence and choose the words that mean the same as the underlined word. Fill in the answer circle under the correct words. Keep working until you come to the word "Stop!" When you come to the word Stop, put your pencils down. Sit quietly until everyone is finished.*

After all children have completed the subtest, **say**: *We have finished this part of the activity.* If no other subtests are to be administered at this time, collect the assessment booklets. If the next subtest is to be administered in this session, continue with the directions.

### VOCABULARY: *Classify/Categorize*

**Objective: Classify words into categories and identify words that fit in given categories**

**Say**: *Look at the Sample at the top of the page. Find the Sample question with some underlined words in it. We will read the Sample question together. Follow along while I read the question aloud.*

### *How are <u>cat</u>, <u>bird</u>, <u>dog</u> the same?*

Then **say**: *Find the sentences under the question. Follow along while I read the sentences aloud.*

### *They are plants.*

### *They are animals.*

### *They are games.*

*Fill in the answer circle by the sentence that tells how the underlined words*

are the same. Are they plants? Are they animals? Are they games? Pause while children mark their answers.

Then **say**: *Which sentence tells how the underlined words are the same?* Call on a child to provide the correct answer.

Then **say**: *Yes, **They are animals** tells how the underlined words are the same. **Cat, bird, and dog are all animals**. You should have filled in the answer circle by **They are animals**. If you did not fill in the correct answer circle, erase your mark and fill in the answer circle by **They are animals**.*

Make sure that children have filled in the correct answer circle. Provide help for children who have difficulty.

Then **say**: *Now I want you to read some more questions that have underlined words in them. First, read each question. Then read the sentences under the question and choose the sentence that tells how the underlined words are the same. Fill in the answer circle by the sentence you choose. Keep working until you come to the word "Stop!" When you come to the word Stop, put your pencils down. Sit quietly until everyone is finished.*

### RESEARCH AND INFORMATION SKILLS: *Alphabetize*

**Objective: Alphabetize to the first letter**

**Say**: *Put your finger by the Sample at the top of the page. Find the two rows of words by the Sample. We will read the two rows of words together. Listen while I read the two rows of words aloud.*

*The first row of words says **dog, pin, ant**.*

*The second row of words says **ant, dog, pin**.*

Harcourt • Reading and Language Skills Assessment

Then **say:** *Look at the three words in the first row of the Sample:* **dog, pin, ant.** *Are these words in ABC order? Now look at the three words in the second row of the Sample:* **ant, dog, pin.** *Are these three words in ABC order? Fill in the answer circle by the row of words that is in ABC order.* Pause while children mark their answers.

Then **say:** *Which row of words is in ABC order—the first row or the second row?* Call on a child to provide the correct answer.

Then **say:** *Yes, the second row of words—ant, dog, pin—is in correct ABC order.* **Ant** *begins with* **a,** *and* **dog** *begins with* **d.** **D** *comes after* **a** *in the alphabet.* **Pin** *begins with* **p.** **P** *comes after* **d** *in the alphabet, so* **pin** *comes last. You should have filled in the answer circle by the second row of words. If you did not fill in the correct answer circle, erase your mark and fill in the answer circle by the second row of words.*

Make sure that children have filled in the correct answer circle. Provide help for children who have difficulty.

Then **say:** *Now I want you to read some more rows of words by yourself. Read each row of words. Then fill in the answer circle by the row that has the words in ABC order. Keep working until you come to the word "Stop!" When you come to the word Stop, put your pencils down. Sit quietly until everyone is finished.*

### LANGUAGE

### Objective: Recognize and use pronouns and describing words

In reading aloud the sentences on this subtest, you may use the word *blank* or simply pause where the tested word is missing.

**Say:** *Find the picture at the top of the page that shows a boy reading a book. Next to the picture is a sentence with a blank in it. The picture will help you figure out which word fits best in the blank. We will read the sentence together. Follow along while I read the sentence aloud.*

_____ **reads a book.**

Then **say:** *Which word fits in the blank to complete the sentence?* **He? or It?** Call on a child to provide the correct answer.

Then **say:** *Yes,* **He** *completes the sentence. Fill in the answer circle under* **He.**

Make sure that children have filled in the correct answer circle. Provide help for children who have difficulty.

Then **say:** *Now I want you to do some more sentences like this. I will tell you what the picture for each sentence shows. Then you will read the sentences and fill in the answer circle under the word that best completes each sentence. If you change your mind after you have marked your answer, erase your mark and fill in the answer circle you do want.*

Continue the test following the same procedures, telling the children what each picture shows. Pause after identifying each picture for children to read the sentences and mark their answer choices independently.

**Say:**

21. *The picture shows two boys throwing a ball. Read the sentence and choose the word that goes in the blank.*
22. *The picture shows a woman taking cookies from an oven. Read the sentence and choose the word that goes in the blank.*
23. *The picture shows a boy standing next to a man. Read the sentence and choose the word that goes in the blank.*

**24.** *The picture shows two girls playing a game. Read the sentence and choose the word that goes in the blank.*

*Say:* Now put your finger by Sample 2. Find the sentence with a blank in it. We will read the sentence together. Follow along while I read the sentence aloud.

> ***I have a _____ coat.***

*There are two words under the sentence. One of the words is a describing word, but the other is **not** a describing word. Which describing word fits in the blank to complete the sentence? **green**? or **hat**? Call on a child to provide the correct answer.*

*Then* **say:** *Yes, **green** completes the sentence. **I have a green coat.** Fill in the answer circle under **green.***

*Make sure that children have filled in the correct answer circle. Provide help for children who have difficulty.*

*Then* **say:** *Now I want you to read the other sentences by yourself. Then fill in the answer circle under the describing word that best completes each sentence. Keep working until you come to the word "Stop." When you come to the word Stop, put your pencil down. Sit quietly until everyone is finished.*

*After all children have completed this subtest,* **say:** *We have finished this activity.* Collect the assessment booklets.

Harcourt • Reading and Language Skills Assessment

# Specific Directions for Administering the *Reading and Language Skills Assessment*

· · · · · · · · · · · · · · · · · · · · · · · · · · · · · · · · · · · · · · · · · ·

## *Time Together*/Book: 1-4
## POSTTEST

### *DECODING: Vowels*

**Objective: Read decodable words with long vowels**

Say: *Put your finger on the picture of the pole in the Sample. Next to the picture you see three words in that row. Find the word that names the picture. Which word is **pole**? Fill in the answer circle under the word **pole**.* Pause while children mark their answers.

Then **say**: *Which word is **pole**?* Call on a child to provide the correct answer.

Then **say**: *Yes, the second word in the row is **pole**, and it names the picture. You should have filled in the answer circle under the second word, **pole**. If you did not fill in the correct answer circle, erase your mark completely and fill in the answer circle under the second word, **pole**.*

Make sure that children have filled in the correct answer circle. Provide help for children who have difficulty.

Then **say**: *Now you will look at some more pictures and fill in the answer circle under the word that names each picture. If you change your mind after you have marked your answer, erase your mark and fill in the answer circle under the word you do want.*

Continue the test following the same procedures, having children find the word that names each picture.

Say:

1. *Find the picture of the **queen**. Which word is **queen**? Fill in the answer circle under the word **queen**.*
2. *Find the picture of **seal**. Which word is **seal**? Fill in the answer circle under the word **seal**.*
3. *Find the picture of a **line**. Which word is **line**? Fill in the answer circle under the word **line**.*
4. *Find the picture of a **ride**. Which word is **ride**? Fill in the answer circle under the word **ride**.*
5. *Find the picture of a **lake**. Which word is **lake**? Fill in the answer circle under the word **lake**.*
6. *Find the picture of **bake**. Which word is **bake**? Fill in the answer circle under the word **bake**.*
7. *Find the picture of a **note**. Which word is **note**? Fill in the answer circle under the word **note**.*
8. *Find the picture of a **mole**. Which word is **mole**? Fill in the answer circle under the word **mole**.*

### *DECODING: Word Structure*

**Objective: Recognize contractions**

Say: *Look at the Sample at the top of the page. Find the sentence with a word underlined. We will read the sentence together. Follow along while I read the sentence aloud.*

**I'll *read the book to you.***

Then **say**: *Look at the underlined word, **I'll**. Read the answer choices under the sentence. Which words under the sentence mean the same as **I'll**?* Call on a child to provide the correct answer.

Then **say**: Yes, *I will means the same as I'll. Fill in the answer circle under the words **I will**.*

Make sure that children have filled in the correct answer circle. Provide help for children who have difficulty.

Then **say**: *Now I want you to read some more sentences by yourself. First, read each sentence with an underlined word. Then read the words under the sentence and choose the words that mean the same as the underlined word. Fill in the answer circle under the correct words. Keep working until you come to the word "Stop!" When you come to the word Stop, put your pencils down. Sit quietly until everyone is finished.*

## VOCABULARY: *Classify/Categorize*

### Objective: Classify words into categories and identify words that fit in given categories

**Say**: *Look at the Sample at the top of the page. Find the Sample question with some underlined words in it. We will read the Sample question together. Follow along while I read the question aloud.*

> ***How are <u>cat</u>, <u>bird</u>, <u>dog</u> the same?***

Then **say**: *Find the sentences under the question. Follow along while I read the sentences aloud.*

> ***They are plants.***
>
> ***They are animals.***
>
> ***They are games.***

*Fill in the answer circle by the sentence that tells how the underlined words are the same. Are they plants? Are they animals? Are they games? Pause while children mark their answers.*

Then **say**: *Which sentence tells how the underlined words are the same? Call on a child to provide the correct answer.*

Then **say**: Yes, *They are animals tells how the underlined words are the same. **Cat, bird, and dog are all animals**. You should have filled in the answer circle by **They are animals**. If you did not fill in the correct answer circle, erase your mark and fill in the answer circle by **They are animals**.*

Make sure that children have filled in the correct answer circle. Provide help for children who have difficulty.

Then **say**: *Now I want you to read some more questions that have underlined words in them. First, read each question. Then read the sentences under the question and choose the sentence that tells how the underlined words are the same. Fill in the answer circle by the sentence you choose. Keep working until you come to the word "Stop!" When you come to the word Stop, put your pencils down. Sit quietly until everyone is finished.*

## RESEARCH AND INFORMATION SKILLS: *Alphabetize*

### Objective: Alphabetize to the first letter

**Say**: *Put your finger by the Sample at the top of the page. Find the two rows of words by the Sample. We will read the two rows of words together. Listen while I read the two rows of words aloud.*

> *The first row of words says **dog, pin, ant**.*
>
> *The second row of words says **ant, dog, pin**.*

Then **say**: *Look at the three words in the first row of the Sample: **dog, pin, ant**. Are these words in ABC order? Now look at the three words in the second row of the Sample: **ant, dog, pin**. Are these three words in ABC order? Fill in the answer circle by the row of words that is in ABC order. Pause while children mark their answers.*

Then **say:** *Which row of words is in ABC order—the first row or the second row?* Call on a child to provide the correct answer.

Then **say:** *Yes, the second row of words—**ant, dog, pin**—is in correct ABC order. **Ant** begins with **a,** and **dog** begins with **d. D** comes after **a** in the alphabet. **Pin** begins with **p. P** comes after **d** in the alphabet, so **pin** comes last. You should have filled in the answer circle by the second row of words. If you did not fill in the correct answer circle, erase your mark and fill in the answer circle by the second row of words.*

Make sure that children have filled in the correct answer circle. Provide help for children who have difficulty.

Then **say:** *Now I want you to read some more rows of words by yourself. Read each row of words. Then fill in the answer circle by the row that has the words in ABC order. Keep working until you come to the word "Stop!" When you come to the word Stop, put your pencils down. Sit quietly until everyone is finished.*

### LANGUAGE

## Objective: Recognize and use pronouns and describing words

In reading aloud the sentences on this subtest, you may use the word *blank* or simply pause where the tested word is missing.

**Say:** *Find the picture at the top of the page that shows a boy reading a book. Next to the picture is a sentence with a blank in it. The picture will help you figure out which word fits best in the blank. We will read the sentence together. Follow along while I read the sentence aloud.*

_____ ***reads a book.***

Then **say:** *Which word fits in the blank to complete the sentence? **He?** or **It?***

Call on a child to provide the correct answer.

Then **say:** *Yes, **He** completes the sentence. Fill in the answer circle under **He.***

Make sure that children have filled in the correct answer circle. Provide help for children who have difficulty.

Then **say:** *Now I want you to do some more sentences like this. I will tell you what the picture for each sentence shows. Then you will read the sentences and fill in the answer circle under the word that best completes each sentence. If you change your mind after you have marked your answer, erase your mark and fill in the answer circle you do want.*

Continue the test following the same procedures, telling the children what each picture shows. Pause after identifying each picture for children to read the sentences and mark their answer choices independently.

**Say:**

21. *The picture shows a woman and a little girl taking cookies from an oven. Read the sentence and choose the word that goes in the blank.*

22. *The picture shows one boy throwing a ball to another boy. Read the sentence and choose the word that goes in the blank.*

23. *The picture shows a man standing next to a boy. Read the sentence and choose the word that goes in the blank.*

24. *The picture shows two girls playing a game. Read the sentence and choose the word that goes in the blank.*

**Say:** *Now put your finger by Sample 2. Find the sentence with a blank in it. We will read the sentence together. Follow along while I read the sentence aloud.*

***I have a _____ coat.***

*There are two words under the sentence. One of the words is a describing word, but the other is **not** a describing word. Which describing word fits in the blank to complete the sentence? **green**? or **hat**?* Call on a child to provide the correct answer.

Then **say:** *Yes, **green** completes the sentence. **I have a green coat**. Fill in the answer circle under **green**.*

Make sure that children have filled in the correct answer circle. Provide help for children who have difficulty.

Then **say:** *Now I want you to read the other sentences by yourself. Then fill in the answer circle under the describing word that best completes each sentence. Keep working until you come to the word "Stop." When you come to the word Stop, put your pencil down. Sit quietly until everyone is finished.*

After all children have completed this subtest, **say:** *We have finished this activity.* Collect the assessment booklets.

Harcourt • Reading and Language Skills Assessment

# Specific Directions for Administering the *Reading and Language Skills Assessment*

●●●●●●●●●●●●●●●●●●●●●●●●●●●●●●●●●●●●●●●●●●●●●●●●●●●●

## *Gather Around*/Book 1-5: PRETEST

### *DECODING: Vowels*

**Objective: Read decodable words with long vowels**

**Say:** *Put your finger on the picture of* **night** *in the Sample. Next to the picture you see three words in that row. Find the word that names the picture. Which word is* **night**? *Fill in the answer circle under the word* **night**. Pause while children mark their answers.

Then **say:** *Which word is* **night**? Call on a child to provide the correct answer.

Then **say:** *Yes, the second word in the row is* **night**, *and it names the picture. You should have filled in the answer circle under the second word,* **night**. *If you did not fill in the correct answer circle, erase your mark and fill in the answer circle under the second word,* **night**.

Make sure that children have filled in the correct answer circle. Provide help for children who have difficulty.

Then **say:** *Now you will look at some more pictures and fill in the answer circle under the word that names each picture. If you change your mind after you have marked your answer, erase your mark and fill in the answer circle under the word you do want.*

Continue the test following the same procedures, having children find the word that names each picture.

**Say:**

1. *Find the picture of a* **nail**. *Which word is* **nail**? *Fill in the answer circle under the word* **nail**.

2. *Find the picture of* **hay**. *Which word is* **hay**? *Fill in the answer circle under the word* **hay**.

3. *Find the picture of a* **light**. *Which word is* **light**? *Fill in the answer circle under the word* **light**.

4. *Find the picture of* **flight**. *Which word is* **flight**? *Fill in the answer circle under the word* **flight**.

5. *Find the picture of a* **mule**. *Which word is* **mule**? *Fill in the answer circle under the word* **mule**.

6. *Find the picture of a* **prune**. *Which word is* **prune**? *Fill in the answer circle under the word* **prune**.

### *DECODING: Inflections*

**Objective: Recognize inflectional endings with spelling changes**

In reading aloud the sentences on this subtest, you may use the word *blank* or simply pause where the tested word is missing.

**Say:** *Look at the Sample at the top of the page. Find the sentence with a blank where a word is missing. We will read the sentence together. Follow along while I read the sentence aloud.*

> *My team is _____ the game.*

Then **say:** *Now read the three words under the sentence. Which word best completes the sentence?* **win**? **wins**? **winning**? Call on a child to provide the correct answer.

Then **say:** *Yes, the word* **winning** *best fits in the blank to complete the sentence.* **My team is winning the game**. *Fill in the answer circle under the word* **winning**.

Then **say:** *Now I want you to read some more sentences that have a word missing. Read the words under the sentences. Then choose the word that best completes each sentence. Keep working until you come to the word "Stop." When you come to the word Stop, put your pencils down. Sit quietly until everyone is finished.*

### DECODING: Contractions

#### Objective: Recognize contractions

**Say:** *Look at the Sample at the top of the page. Find the sentence with a word underlined. We will read the sentence together. Follow along while I read the sentence aloud.*

> **I've got a new book.**

Then **say:** *Look at the underlined word, **I've**. Which words mean the same as **I've**?* Call on a child to provide the correct answer.

Then **say:** *Yes, **I have** means the same as **I've**. Fill in the answer circle under the words **I have**.*

Then **say:** *Now I want you to read some more sentences by yourself. First, read each sentence with an underlined word. Then read the words under the sentence and choose the words that mean the same as the underlined word. Fill in the answer circle under the correct words. Keep working until you come to the word "Stop." When you come to the word Stop, put your pencils down. Sit quietly until everyone is finished.*

### COMPREHENSION: Plot

#### Objective: Identify and describe the element of plot in a story as well as the story's beginning and ending

**Say:** *Put your finger by the Sample at the top of the page. Find the short story called "Carl Finds a Dog." We will read the story together. Follow along while I read the story aloud.*

> **Carl saw a little dog in the yard.**
>
> **He called to the dog, and the dog came.**
>
> **The dog looked happy to see Carl.**
>
> **Carl petted the dog and gave him some water.**

Then **say:** *Now find the question under the Sample story. Follow along while I read the question aloud. **What happens at the beginning of this story? Carl petted the dog? Carl gave the dog water? Carl saw a dog in the yard?*** Call on a child to provide the correct answer.

Then **say:** *Yes, at the beginning of the story, **Carl saw a dog in the yard**. Fill in the answer circle by **Carl saw a dog in the yard**.*

Make sure that children have filled in the correct answer circle. Provide help for children who have difficulty.

Then **say:** *Now I want you to read a longer story and answer the questions about the story by yourself. Keep working until you come to the word "Stop." When you come to the word Stop, put your pencils down. Sit quietly until everyone is finished.*

### COMPREHENSION: Main Idea

#### Objective: Recognize main idea in a passage

**Say:** *Put your finger by the Sample at the top of the page. Find the short story called "Going to School." We will read the story together. Follow along while I read the story aloud.*

> **Rose likes school.**
>
> **She has a lot of friends there.**
>
> **She reads books at school.**
>
> **She plays games.**
>
> **She learns so much.**

Harcourt • Reading and Language Skills Assessment

Then **say:** *Now find the question under the Sample story. Follow along while I read the question aloud.* **What is this story mostly about? Rose likes school? Rose reads books at school? Rose plays games?** *Call on a child to provide the correct answer.*

Then **say:** *Yes, this story is mostly about* **Rose likes school.** *Fill in the answer circle by* **Rose likes school.**

Make sure that children have filled in the correct answer circle. Provide help for children who have difficulty.

Then **say:** *Now I want you to read four more stories and answer the questions by yourself. Keep working until you come to the word "Stop." When you come to the word Stop, put your pencils down. Sit quietly until everyone is finished.*

### LANGUAGE: Verbs

### Objective: Recognize action words

**Say:** *Put your finger by the Sample. Find the sentence with some words under it. We will read the sentence together. Follow along while I read the sentence aloud.*

*Two ducks quacked.*

Then **say:** *Which word is the verb from the sentence?* **Two? ducks? quacked?** *Call on a child to provide the correct answer.*

Then **say:** *Yes,* **quacked** *is the verb that tells about the past in this sentence. Fill in the answer circle by* **quacked.**

Make sure that children have filled in the correct answer circle. Provide help for children who have difficulty.

Then **say:** *Now I want you to read some more sentences and answer the questions by yourself. You will fill in the answer circle by the verb from each sentence. The verb might tell about now, or it might tell about the past. Keep working until you come to the word "Stop." When you come to the word Stop, put your pencils down. Sit quietly until everyone is finished.*

After all children have completed the subtest, **say:** *We have finished this activity.* Collect the assessment booklets.

# Specific Directions for Administering the *Reading and Language Skills Assessment*

● ● ● ● ● ● ● ● ● ● ● ● ● ● ● ● ● ● ● ● ● ● ● ● ● ● ● ● ● ● ● ● ● ● ● ● ● ● ● ● ● ● ● ● ● ● ● ● ● ● ● ● ● ●

*Gather Around/Book 1-5:*
POSTTEST

### DECODING: *Vowels*

Objective: Read decodable words with long vowels

**Say:** *Put your finger on the picture of* **night** *in the Sample. Next to the picture you see three words in that row. Find the word that names the picture. Which word is* **night**? *Fill in the answer circle under the word* **night**. Pause while children mark their answers.

Then **say:** *Which word is* **night**? Call on a child to provide the correct answer.

Then **say:** *Yes, the second word in the row is* **night**, *and it names the picture. You should have filled in the answer circle under the second word,* **night**. *If you did not fill in the correct answer circle, erase your mark and fill in the answer circle under the second word,* **night**.

Make sure that children have filled in the correct answer circle. Provide help for children who have difficulty.

Then **say:** *Now you will look at some more pictures and fill in the answer circle under the word that names each picture. If you change your mind after you have marked your answer, erase your mark and fill in the answer circle under the word you do want.*

Continue the test following the same procedures, having children find the word that names each picture.

**Say:**

1. *Find the picture of* **paint**. *Which word is* **paint**? *Fill in the answer circle under*
the word **paint**.

2. *Find the picture of a* **tray**. *Which word is* **tray**? *Fill in the answer circle under the word* **tray**.

3. *Find the picture of* **right**. *Which word is* **right**? *Fill in the answer circle under the word* **right**.

4. *Find the picture of* **light**. *Which word is* **light**? *Fill in the answer circle under the word* **light**.

5. *Find the picture of a* **cube**. *Which word is* **cube**? *Fill in the answer circle under the word* **cube**.

6. *Find the picture of a* **tube**. *Which word is* **tube**? *Fill in the answer circle under the word* **tube**.

### DECODING: *Inflections*

Objective: Recognize inflectional endings with spelling changes

In reading aloud the sentences on this subtest, you may use the word *blank* or simply pause where the tested word is missing.

**Say:** *Look at the Sample at the top of the page. Find the sentence with a blank where a word is missing. We will read the sentence together. Follow along while I read the sentence aloud.*

**My team is _____ the game.**

Then **say:** *Now read the three words under the sentence. Which word best completes the sentence?* **win? wins? winning?** Call on a child to provide the correct answer.

Then **say:** *Yes, the word* **winning** *best fits in the blank to complete the sentence.* **My team is winning the game.** *Fill in the answer circle under the word*

Harcourt • Reading and Language Skills Assessment

*winning.*

Then **say:** *Now I want you to read some more sentences that have a word missing. Read the words under the sentences. Then choose the word that best completes each sentence. Keep working until you come to the word "Stop." When you come to the word Stop, put your pencils down. Sit quietly until everyone is finished.*

### DECODING: *Contractions*

**Objective: Recognize contractions**

**Say:** *Look at the Sample at the top of the page. Find the sentence with a word underlined. We will read the sentence together. Follow along while I read the sentence aloud.*

> **I've got a new book.**

Then **say:** *Look at the underlined word,* **I've.** *Which words mean the same as* **I've?** Call on a child to provide the correct answer.

Then **say:** *Yes,* **I have** *means the same as* **I've.** *Fill in the answer circle under the words* **I have.**

Then **say:** *Now I want you to read some more sentences by yourself. First, read each sentence with an underlined word. Then read the words under the sentence and choose the words that mean the same as the underlined word. Fill in the answer circle under the correct words. Keep working until you come to the word "Stop." When you come to the word Stop, put your pencils down. Sit quietly until everyone is finished.*

### COMPREHENSION: *Plot*

**Objective: Identify and describe the element of plot in a story as well as the story's beginning and ending**

**Say:** *Put your finger by the Sample at the top of the page. Find the short story called "Carl Finds a Dog." We will read*

*the story together. Follow along while I read the story aloud.*

> **Carl saw a little dog in the yard.**
>
> **He called to the dog, and the dog came.**
>
> **The dog looked happy to see Carl.**
>
> **Carl petted the dog and gave him some water.**

Then **say:** *Now find the question under the Sample story. Follow along while I read the question aloud.* **What happens at the beginning of this story? Carl petted the dog? Carl gave the dog water? Carl saw a dog in the yard?** Call on a child to provide the correct answer.

Then **say:** *Yes, at the beginning of the story,* **Carl saw a dog in the yard.** *Fill in the answer circle by* **Carl saw a dog in the yard.**

Make sure that children have filled in the correct answer circle. Provide help for children who have difficulty.

Then **say:** *Now I want you to read a longer story and answer the questions about the story by yourself. Keep working until you come to the word "Stop." When you come to the word Stop, put your pencils down. Sit quietly until everyone is finished.*

### COMPREHENSION: *Main Idea*

**Objective: Recognize main idea in a passage**

**Say:** *Put your finger by the Sample at the top of the page. Find the short story called "Going to School." We will read the story together. Follow along while I read the story aloud.*

> **Rose likes school.**
>
> **She has a lot of friends there.**
>
> **She reads books at school.**
>
> **She plays games.**
>
> **She learns so much.**

Then **say:** *Now find the question under the Sample story. Follow along while I read the question aloud.* **What is this story mostly about? Rose likes school? Rose reads books at school? Rose plays games?** *Call on a child to provide the correct answer.*

Then **say:** *Yes, this story is mostly about* **Rose likes school.** *Fill in the answer circle by* **Rose likes school.**

Make sure that children have filled in the correct answer circle. Provide help for children who have difficulty.

Then **say:** *Now I want you to read four more stories and answer the questions by yourself. Keep working until you come to the word "Stop." When you come to the word Stop, put your pencils down. Sit quietly until everyone is finished.*

### LANGUAGE: Verbs

**Objective: Recognize action words**

**Say:** *Put your finger by the Sample. Find the sentence with some words under it.*

*We will read the sentence together. Follow along while I read the sentence aloud.*

**Two ducks quacked.**

Then **say:** *Which word is the verb from the sentence?* **Two? ducks? quacked?** *Call on a child to provide the correct answer.*

Then **say:** *Yes,* **quacked** *is the verb that tells about the past in this sentence. Fill in the answer circle by* **quacked.**

Make sure that children have filled in the correct answer circle. Provide help for children who have difficulty.

Then **say:** *Now I want you to read some more sentences and answer the questions by yourself. You will fill in the answer circle by the verb from each sentence. The verb might tell about now, or it might tell about the past. Keep working until you come to the word "Stop." When you come to the word Stop, put your pencils down. Sit quietly until everyone is finished.*

After all children have completed the subtest, **say:** *We have finished this activity.* Collect the assessment booklets.

Harcourt • Reading and Language Skills Assessment

### Scoring and Interpreting the Assessments

The *Reading and Language Skills Assessment* can be scored using the answer keys. Follow these steps:

1. Turn to the appropriate answer key in the Appendix.
2. Compare the student's responses, item by item, to the answer key and put a check mark next to each item that is correctly answered.
3. Count the number of correct responses for each skill or subtest and write this number on the "Pupil Score" line on the booklet cover. Add the Pupil Scores for each skill to obtain the Total Score.
4. Determine if the child met the criterion for each skill.

A child who scores at or above the criterion level for each subtest is considered competent in that skill area and is probably ready to move forward without additional practice. A column for writing comments about "Pupil Strength" has been provided on the cover of the assessment booklet.

A child who does not reach criterion level probably needs additional instruction and/or practice in that particular skill. Examine the child's scores for each subtest and decide whether you should reteach a particular skill, or move forward to the next theme.

For teachers who wish to keep a cumulative record of Pupil Scores across books, a Student Record Form has been provided for that purpose in the Appendix.

A *Reading and Language Skills Assessment* is just one observation of a child's reading behavior. It should be combined with other evidence of a child's progress, such as the teacher's daily observations, student work samples, and individual reading conferences. The sum of all of this information, coupled with test scores, is more reliable and valid than any single piece of information.

# Mid-Year and End-of-Year Reading and Language Skills Assessments

························································

## Description of the Assessments

The *Mid-Year* and *End-of-Year Reading and Language Skills Assessments* are criterion-referenced tests designed to measure children's achievement on the skills taught in the themes. The assessments evaluate achievement in decoding/phonics, vocabulary, research and information skills, comprehension, and language. The assessments are designed to give a global picture of how well children apply the skills taught in the program. They are not intended to be diagnostic tests and do not yield specific scores for each skill. However, if a child does not reach the overall criterion for the total test, it is possible to judge his or her performance on the major skill categories (e.g., decoding/phonics, vocabulary, and comprehension).

The formats used on the *Mid-Year* and *End-of-Year Reading and Language Skills Assessments* follow the same style as those used in instruction. This ensures that the assessments are aligned with the instruction.

## Contents of the Assessments

The following tables list the contents of the *Mid-Year* and *End-of-Year Assessments*. The content of the *Mid-Year Reading and Language Skills Assessment* comes from the skills taught in Books 1-1, 1-2, and 1-3. The content of the *End-of-Year Reading and Language Skills Assessment* comes from the skills taught in Books 1-1 through 1-5.

## Scheduling the Assessments

The *Mid-Year* and *End-of-Year Reading and Language Skills Assessments* have been designed to correlate with specific skills introduced and reinforced within each book of the program. Each major reading skill taught in the program is represented on the assessments. The *Mid-Year* and *End-of-Year Reading Skills Assessments* are summative tests. That is, they are designed to evaluate whether children can apply the skills learned.

The *Mid-Year Reading and Language Skills Assessment* may be given after a child has completed the first three books at this grade level. The *End-of-Year Reading and Language Skills Assessment* may be given after a child has completed all five books at this grade level.

The *Mid-Year* and *End-of-Year Reading and Language Skills Assessments* should be given in one session, if possible. The pace at which you administer the assessments will depend on your particular class and group. The assessments are not timed. Most children should be able to complete each assessment in approximately thirty to forty-five minutes.

## Mid-Year Reading and Language Skills Assessment

| Skill Category | Subcategory | Objective | Items |
|---|---|---|---|
| Decoding/Phonics | Phonemes | Distinguish short, long, and *R*-controlled vowel sounds (/a/*a*; /i/*i*; /o/*o*; /e/*e*; /u/*u*; /ō/ *ow, oa*; /ôr/*or*, *ore*; /är/*ar*; /ûr/*er, ir, ur*) | 1–9 |
| Decoding/Phonics | Decodable Words | Read decodable words with short, long, and R-controlled vowel sounds (/a/*a*; /i/*i*; /o/*o*; /e/*e*; /u/*u*; /ō/*ow, oa*; /ôr/*or*, *ore*; /är/*ar*; /ûr/*er, ir, ur*) | 10–18 |
| Decoding/Phonics | Blends | Decode words with initial consonant blends (*r, s, l*) | 19–24 |
| Decoding/Phonics | Digraphs | Decode words with consonants digraphs (/k/*ck*; /th/ *th*; /sh/*sh*; /ch/*ch*; /kw/*qu*, /hw/*wh*) | 25–30 |
| Decoding/Phonics | Inflections | Decode words with inflectional endings (*-s, -ed, -ing*, no spelling change) | 31–34 |
| Comprehension | Sequence | Recognize and analyze text that is presented in sequential or chronological order | 37, 42 |
| Comprehension | Setting | Recognize when and where events take place in a narrative | 35, 39 |
| Comprehension | Character | Identify main characters in a narrative | 38, 41 |
| Comprehension | Details | Recognize important details in a passage | 36, 40 |
| Language | | Display command of standard English conventions | 43–50 |

## End-of-Year Reading and Language Skills Assessment

| Skill Category | Subcategory | Objective | Items |
|---|---|---|---|
| Decoding/Phonics | Decodable Words | Read decodable words with long and R-controlled vowel sounds (/ē/e, ee, ea; /ā/a-e; /ī/i-e; /ō/o-e; /ī/igh; /ā/ai, ay; /ōō/u-e; /är/ar; /ûr/er, ir, ur) | 1–12 |
| Decoding/Phonics | Inflectional Endings | Decode words with inflectional endings (-ed, -ing, with spelling changes) | 13–16 |
| Decoding/Phonics | Contractions | Decode words with contractions ('ll, n't, 's, 'd, 've, 're) | 17–22 |
| Vocabulary | Classify/ Categorize | Classify words into categories | 23–26 |
| Research and Information Skills | Alphabetize | Alphabetize to the first letter | 27–30 |
| Comprehension | Plot | Identify and describe the element of plot in a story | 31, 36 |
| Comprehension | Main Idea | Identify the main idea in a passage | 37–38 |
| Comprehension | Details | Identify important details in a passage | 35 |
| Comprehension | Character | Identify main characters in a narrative | 33 |
| Comprehension | Sequence | Recognize and analyze text that is presented in sequential or chronological order | 34 |
| Comprehension | Setting | Recognize when and where events take place in a narrative | 32 |
| Language | | Display command of standard English conventions | 39–48 |

Harcourt • Reading and Language Skills Assessment

# Directions for Administering the *Mid-Year Reading and Language Skills Assessment*

● ● ● ● ● ● ● ● ● ● ● ● ● ● ● ● ● ● ● ● ● ● ● ● ● ● ● ● ● ● ● ● ● ● ● ● ● ● ● ● ● ● ● ● ● ● ● ● ●

*(Assessing skills taught in Books 1-1, 1-2, and 1-3)*

## DECODING: *Vowels* (Items 1–9)

**Objective: Identify and isolate the medial phoneme of a spoken word (short, long, and *R*-controlled vowels)**

**Say:** *Put your finger by the Sample. Look at the three pictures. I will tell you a sound to listen for. Then I will name the three pictures while you listen carefully. Choose the picture whose name has the sound I tell you. Which picture has the /a/ sound? rope? can? geese? Fill in the answer circle under the picture that has the /a/ sound.* Pause while children mark their answers.

Then **say:** *Which picture has the /a/ sound?* Call on a child to provide the correct answer.

Then **say:** *Yes, **can** has the /a/ sound. You should have filled in the answer circle under the picture of the **can**.*

Make sure that children have filled in the correct answer circle. Provide help for children who have difficulty.

Then **say:** *Now you will look at some more pictures and choose the pictures that have the sounds I tell you. Fill in the answer circle under the pictures you choose.*

Continue the test following the same procedures, first having children listen for a specific phoneme, and then having them find the picture that has that phoneme.

Say:

1. *Which picture has the /i/ sound? soap? sit? cake? Find the picture whose name has the /i/ sound.*
2. *Which picture has the /a/ sound? cap? ice? goat? Find the picture whose name has the /a/ sound.*
3. *Which picture has the /o/ sound? tack? fly? hop? Find the picture whose name has the /o/ sound.*
4. *Which picture has the /u/ sound? chick? run? feet? Find the picture whose name has the /u/ sound.*
5. *Which picture has the /e/ sound? stop? hole? bed? Find the picture whose name has the /e/ sound.*
6. *Which picture has the /ō/ sound? boat? price? ship? Find the picture whose name has the /ō/ sound.*
7. *Which picture has the /ûr/ sound? skirt? tray? cone? Find the picture whose name has the /ûr/ sound.*
8. *Which picture has the /ôr/ sound? kick? fork? shell? Find the picture whose name has the /ôr/ sound.*
9. *Which picture has the /är/ sound? bus? jar? sheep? Find the picture whose name has the /är/ sound.*

## DECODING: *Vowels* (Items 10–18)

**Objective: Read decodable words with short, long, and *R*-controlled vowels**

**Say:** *Put your finger on the picture of the **pet** in the Sample. Next to the picture you see three words in a row. Find the word that names the picture. Which word is **pet**? Fill in the answer circle under the word **pet**.* Pause while children mark their answers.

Then **say:** *Which word is pet?* Call on a child to provide the correct answer.

Then **say:** *Yes, the first word in the row is **pet**, and it names the picture. You should have filled in the answer circle under the first word, **pet**.*

Make sure that children have filled in the correct answer circle. Provide help for children who have difficulty.

Then **say:** *Now you will look at some more pictures and fill in the answer circle under the word that names each picture.*

Continue the test following the same procedures, having children find the word that names each picture.

**Say:**

10. *Find the picture of a **hill**. Which word is **hill**? Fill in the answer circle under the word **hill**.*

11. *Find the picture of a **man**. Which word is **man**? Fill in the answer circle under the word **man**.*

12. *Find the picture of a **coat**. Which word is **coat**? Fill in the answer circle under the word **coat**.*

13. *Find the picture of a **top**. Which word is **top**? Fill in the answer circle under the word **top**.*

14. *Find the picture of a **mess**. Which word is **mess**? Fill in the answer circle under the word **mess**.*

15. *Find the picture of a **nut**. Which word is **nut**? Fill in the answer circle under the word **nut**.*

16. *Find the picture of a **horn**. Which word is **horn**? Fill in the answer circle under the word **horn**.*

17. *Find the picture of a **barn**. Which word is **barn**? Fill in the answer circle under the word **barn**.*

18. *Find the picture of a **bird**. Which word is **bird**? Fill in the answer circle under the word **bird**.*

## DECODING: Blends and Digraphs
*(Items 19–30)*

### Objective: Recognize sound-letter relationships of initial and final blends and digraphs

In administering this subtest, do not name the letters for the children or say the sounds the letters make.

**Say:** *Put your finger by the Sample. Look at the letters. Next to the letters you see three pictures. I will name the three pictures for you. Choose the picture whose name **begins** with the sounds the letters stand for. Look at the letters in the Sample. Which picture name begins with the sounds those letters stand for? frog? fox? rope? Fill in the answer circle under the picture name that begins with the sounds the letters stand for.* Pause while children mark their answers.

Then **say:** *Which picture name begins with the sounds the letters stand for?* Call on a child to provide the correct answer.

Then **say:** *Yes, **frog** begins with the same sounds the letters stand for in the Sample. You should have filled in the answer circle under the picture of the **frog**.*

Make sure that children have filled in the correct answer circle. Provide help for children who have difficulty.

Then **say:** *Now you will look at some more letters and choose the picture names that begin with the sounds the letters stand for. Fill in the answer circle under the pictures you choose.*

Continue the test following the same procedures, first having children look at the letters, and then having them find the picture names that begin with the sounds the letters stand for.

Harcourt • Reading and Language Skills Assessment

19. *Look at the letters. Which picture name begins with the sounds the letters stand for? mat? smell? sled?*

20. *Look at the letters. Which picture name begins with the sounds the letters stand for? tiger? school? store?*

21. *Look at the letters. Which picture name begins with the sounds the letters stand for? toy? rock? trash?*

22. *Look at the letters. Which picture name begins with the sounds the letters stand for? razor? crab? cut?*

23. *Look at the letters. Which picture name begins with the sounds the letters stand for? blow? lamp? book?*

24. *Look at the letters. Which picture name begins with the sounds the letters stand for? light? grab? glass?*

25. *Look at the letters. Which picture name begins with the sounds the letters stand for? bag? dress? quack?*

26. *Look at the letters. Which picture name begins with the sounds the letters stand for? web? wheat? hoe?*

Then **say**: *Now find the Sample at the top of the next page. Put your finger by the Sample. Look at the letters and the three pictures next to the letters. This time, fill in the answer circle under the picture whose name **ends** with the sounds the letters stand for. Look at the letters in the Sample. Which picture name **ends** with the sounds the letters stand for? key? sink? mask? Fill in the answer circle under the picture name that **ends** with the sounds the letters stand for.* Pause while children mark their answers.

Then **say**: *Which picture name ends with the same sounds the letters stand for in the Sample?* Call on a child to provide the correct answer.

Then **say**: *Yes, **mask** ends with the same sounds the letters stand for in the*

*Sample. You should have filled in the answer circle under the picture of the **mask**.*

Make sure that children have filled in the correct answer circle. Provide help for children who have difficulty.

Then **say**: *Now you will look at some more letters and choose the picture names that end with the sounds the letters stand for. Fill in the answer circle under the pictures you choose.*

Continue the test following the same procedures, first having children look at the letters, and then having them find the picture names that end with the sounds the letters stand for.

27. *Look at the letters. Which picture name ends with the sounds the letters stand for? lock? tub? jam?*

28. *Look at the letters. Which picture name ends with the sounds the letters stand for? pail? fish? dress?*

29. *Look at the letters. Which picture name ends with the sounds the letters stand for? bath? fire? horse?*

30. *Look at the letters. Which picture name ends with the sounds the letters stand for? kick? lunch? push?*

### DECODING: *Word Structure*
(Items 31–34)

#### Objective: Recognize inflectional endings with no spelling changes

In reading aloud the sentences on this subtest, you may use the word *blank* or simply pause where the tested word is missing.

**Say**: *Look at the Sample at the top of the page. You see a sentence with a blank where a word is missing. There are three words under the sentence. I will read the sentence to you. You will read the words under the sentence. Then you will choose the word that best completes the sentence. The Sample sentence says:*

**She _____ the box.**

Now read the three words under the sentence. Which word makes sense in the sentence? Fill in the answer circle under the word that best completes the sentence. Pause while children mark their answers.

Then **say**: *Which word best completes the sentence?* Call on a child to provide the correct answer.

Then **say**: *Yes, the word **packed** best fits in the blank to complete the sentence. **She packed the box.** You should have filled in the answer circle under the word **packed**.*

Then **say**: *Now I will read you some more sentences that have a word missing. Read the words under the sentences. Then choose the word that best completes each sentence.*

Continue the test following the same procedures, first reading each sentence aloud to the children, then pausing while they choose the word that completes each sentence.

**Say:**

31. *The sentence in this row says: **The plant is _____.** Find the word that best completes the sentence.*

32. *The sentence in this row says: **She _____ her drink.** Find the word that best completes the sentence.*

33. *The sentence in this row says: **Dan is _____ a book.** Find the word that best completes the sentence.*

34. *The sentence in this row says: **She _____ me pick up sticks.** Find the word that best completes the sentence.*

**COMPREHENSION: *Sequence, Details, Setting, Character*** *(Items 35–42)*

**Objective: Recognize sequence of events; recognize important details in a passage; identify and describe the**
elements of setting and character in a story

Directions: Tell children to find the sample at the top of the page.

**Say:** *Put your finger by the Sample at the top of the page. Find the short story called "Growing a Plant." We will read the story together. Follow along while I read the story aloud.*

**Here is how to grow a plant.**

**Put the plant in the sun.**

**Give the plant a drink every day.**

**Watch the plant grow.**

Then **say**: *Find the question under the Sample story: Follow along while I read the question aloud. **What should you do first? Watch the plant grow? Put the plant in the sun? Give the plant a drink?** Call on a child to provide the correct answer.*

Then **say**: *Yes, first you should **Put the plant in the sun.** Fill in the answer circle by **Put the plant in the sun.** Pause while children mark their answers.*

Make sure that children have filled in the correct answer circle. Provide help for children who have difficulty.

Then **say**: *Now I want you to read two more stories and answer the questions by yourself. Keep working until you come to the word "Stop."*

**LANGUAGE: *Sentences*** *(Items 43–46)*

**Objective: Recognize correct word order; recognize asking and telling sentences**

Directions: Tell children to find Sample 1 at the top of the page.

**Say:** *Put your finger by Sample 1. You see some words with **Yes** and **No** under them. I will read the words to you. Decide whether the words are in the correct order to make a sentence. The words by Sample 1 say:*

Harcourt • Reading and Language Skills Assessment

*my cat? Where is*

*If the words are in the correct order to make a sentence, fill in the answer circle under* **Yes.** *If the words are not in the correct order to make a sentence, fill in the circle under* **No.** *Pause while children mark their answers.*

Then **say:** *Are the words in the correct order to make a sentence?* Call on a child to provide the correct answer.

Then **say:** *No, the words are not in the correct order. You should have filled in the answer circle under* **No.**

Make sure that children have filled in the correct answer circle. Provide help for children who have difficulty.

Then **say:** *Now I will read you some more words. If the words are in the correct order to make a sentence, fill in the answer circle under* **Yes.** *If the words are not in the correct order, fill in the answer circle under* **No.**

Continue the test following the same procedures, having children determine whether the words are in the correct order to make a sentence. Pause after reading each question so that children can mark their answers.

**Say:**

**43.** *The words in this row say:* **She is my friend.** *Fill in the answer circle under* **Yes** *or* **No.**

**44.** *The words in this row say:* **go with me? Who will** *Fill in the answer circle under* **Yes** *or* **No.**

Tell children to find Sample 2. **Say:** *Put your finger by Sample 2. You see a sentence with a period and a question mark under it. I will read the sentence to you. Decide whether it is a telling or an asking sentence The sentence in Sample 2 says:*.

**Will you come now**

*Is that a telling or an asking sentence? Fill in the answer circle under the period if* **Will you come now** *is a telling sentence. Fill in the answer circle under the question mark if* **Will you come now** *is an asking sentence. Pause while children mark their answers.*

Then **say:** *Is* **Will you come now** *a telling or an asking sentence?* Call on a child to provide the correct answer.

Then **say:** *Yes,* **Will you come now** *asks a question. You should have filled in the answer circle under the question mark.*

Make sure that children have filled in the correct answer circle. Provide help for children who have difficulty.

Then **say:** *Now I will read you some more sentences. Choose the correct end mark for each sentence.*

Continue the test following the same procedures, having children determine the end mark for each sentence. Pause after reading each question so that children can mark their answers.

**Say:**

**45.** *The sentence in this row says:* **I like to eat plums** *Choose the correct end mark.*

**46.** *The sentence in this row says:* **Do you want to ride the horse** *Choose the correct end mark.*

### LANGUAGE: *Parts of Sentences*
*(Items 47–48)*

### Objective: Recognize naming and telling parts of sentences

**Say:** *Put your finger by the Sample. You see a sentence with a word underlined in it. I will read the sentence to you. Decide whether the underlined word is the naming part of the sentence or the telling part of the sentence. The Sample sentence says:*

Harcourt • Reading and Language Skills Assessment

**_Sam_ hits the ball.**

_**Sam** is underlined. Is **Sam** the naming part or the telling part of the sentence? Fill in the answer circle under naming part or telling part._ Pause while children mark their answers. If you feel it is necessary, familiarize children with the terms **naming part** and **telling part**. Write the words on a chalkboard and identify them for the children.

Then **say:** _Is **Sam** the naming or the telling part of the sentence?_ Call on a child to provide the correct answer.

Then **say:** _Yes, **Sam** is the naming part. You should have filled in the answer circle under **naming part**._

Make sure that children have filled in the correct answer circle. Provide help for children who have difficulty.

Then **say:** _Now I will read you two more sentences. Part of each sentence is underlined. Decide whether the underlined word or words are the naming or telling part of each sentence._

Continue the test following the same procedures, having children determine whether the underlined words are the naming or telling part of each sentence. Pause after reading each question so that children can mark their answers.

**Say:**

47. _The sentence in this row says: **Jim and Ann** <u>are my best friends</u>. Is **Jim and Ann** the naming or telling part of the sentence? Mark your answer._

48. _The sentence in this row says: **The cat** <u>sees a fish</u>. Is sees a fish the naming or telling part of the sentence? Mark your answer._

**LANGUAGE: Nouns** _(Items 49–50)_

**Objective: Recognize nouns**

**Say:** _Put your finger by the Sample. Find the sentence with some words under it. Listen while I read the sentence to you._

**_He will **pick up** the rock._**

_Find the words under the sentence. Fill in the answer circle by the noun that names a person, a place, an animal, or a thing._ Pause while children mark their answers.

Then **say:** _Which word names a noun?_ Call on a child to provide the correct answer.

Then **say:** _Yes, **rock** is a noun that names a thing. You should have filled in the answer circle by **rock**. If you did not fill in the correct answer circle, erase your mark and fill in the answer circle by **rock**._

Make sure that children have filled in the correct answer circle. Provide help for children who have difficulty.

Then **say:** _Now we will read some more sentences. Follow along while I read each sentence aloud. Then read the answer choices under each sentence and choose the word that names a person, a place, an animal, or a thing._

Continue the test following the same procedures, reading aloud the sentences for each question. Pause after reading each sentence for children to read the answer choices independently and mark their answers.

**Say:**

49. _The sentence in this row says: **We saw a mouse in the house.** Choose the noun that names a person, a place, an animal, or a thing._

50. _The sentence in this row says: **Our house in on West Street.** Choose the noun that names a person, a place, an animal, or a thing._

Harcourt • Reading and Language Skills Assessment

# Directions for Administering the *End-of-Year Reading and Language Skills Assessment*

................................................................

(Assessing skills taught in *Books 1-1* through *1-5*)

### DECODING: *Vowels* (Items 1–12)

**Objective: Read decodable words with long and r-controlled vowels**

**Say:** *Put your finger on the picture of the pole in the Sample. Next to the picture you see three words in that row. Find the word that names the picture. Which word is* **pole**? *Fill in the answer circle under the word* **pole.** Pause while children mark their answers.

Then **say:** *Which word is* **pole**? Call on a child to provide the correct answer.

Then **say:** *Yes, the second word in the row is* **pole,** *and it names the picture. You should have filled in the answer circle under the second word,* **pole.**

Make sure that children have filled in the correct answer circle. Provide help for children who have difficulty.

Then **say:** *Now you will look at some more pictures and fill in the answer circle under the word that names each picture.*

Continue the test following the same procedures, having children find the word that names each picture.

**Say:**

1. *Find the picture of the* **sheep**. *Which word is* **sheep**? *Fill in the answer circle under the word* **sheep.**
2. *Find the picture of* **read**. *Which word is* **read**? *Fill in the answer circle under the word* **read.**
3. *Find the picture of* **skate**. *Which word is* **skate**? *Fill in the answer circle under the word* **skate.**
4. *Find the picture of a* **nail**. *Which word is* **nail**? *Fill in the answer circle under the word* **nail.**
5. *Find the picture of* **hay**. *Which word is* **hay**? *Fill in the answer circle under the word* **hay.**
6. *Find the picture of a* **light**. *Which word is* **light**? *Fill in the answer circle under the word* **light.**
7. *Find the picture of a* **dome**. *Which word is* **dome**? *Fill in the answer circle under the word* **dome.**
8. *Find the picture of a* **bike**. *Which word is* **bike**? *Fill in the answer circle under the word* **bike.**
9. *Find the picture of a* **prune**. *Which word is* **prune**? *Fill in the answer circle under the word* **prune.**
10. *Find the picture of a* **crow**. *Which word is* **crow**? *Fill in the answer circle under the word* **crow.**
11. *Find the picture of a* **barn**. *Which word is* **barn**? *Fill in the answer circle under the word* **barn.**
12. *Find the picture of* **third**. *Which word is* **third**? *Fill in the answer circle under the word* **third.**

### DECODING: *Inflections* (Items 13–16)

**Objective: Recognize inflectional endings with spelling changes**

In reading aloud the sentences on this subtest, you may use the word *blank* or simply pause where the tested word is missing.

Harcourt • Reading and Language Skills Assessment

**Say:** *Look at the Sample at the top of the page. Find the sentence with a blank where a word is missing. We will read the sentence together. Follow along while I read the sentence aloud.*

> **My favorite team is _____ the game.**

Then **say:** *Now read the three words under the sentence. Which word best completes the sentence?* **win? wins? winning?** Call on a child to provide the correct answer.

Then **say:** *Yes, the word* **winning** *best fits in the blank to complete the sentence.* **My favorite team is winning the game.** *Fill in the answer circle under the word* **winning.**

Then **say:** *Now I want you to read some more sentences that have a word missing. Read the words under the sentences. Then choose the word that best completes each sentence. Keep working until you come to the word "Stop."*

### DECODING: Contractions
*(Items 17–22)*

#### Objective: Recognize contractions

**Say:** *Look at the Sample at the top of the page. Find the sentence with a word underlined. We will read the sentence together. Follow along while I read the sentence aloud.*

> **I'll read the book to you.**

Then **say:** *Look at the underlined word,* **I'll.** *Read the answer choices under the sentence. Which words under the sentence mean the same as* **I'll?** Call on a child to provide the correct answer.

Then **say:** *Yes,* **I will** *means the same as* **I'll.** *Fill in the answer circle under the words* **I will.**

Make sure that children have filled in the correct answer circle. Provide help for children who have difficulty.

Then **say:** *Now I want you to read some more sentences by yourself. First, read each sentence with an underlined word. Then read the words under the sentence and choose the words that mean the same as the underlined word. Fill in the answer circle under the correct words. Keep working until you come to the word "Stop."*

### VOCABULARY: Classify/Categorize
*(23–26)*

#### Objective: Classify words into categories and identify words that fit in given categories

**Say:** *Look at the Sample at the top of the page. Find the Sample question with some underlined words in it. We will read the Sample question together. Follow along while I read the question aloud.*

> **How are <u>cat</u>, <u>bird</u>, <u>dog</u> the same?**

Then **say:** *Find the sentences under the question. Follow along while I read the sentences aloud.*

> **They are plants.**
>
> **They are animals.**
>
> **They are games.**

*Fill in the answer circle by the sentence that tells how the underlined words are the same. Are they plants? Are they animals? Are they games?* Pause while children mark their answers.

Then **say:** *Which sentence tells how the underlined words are the same?* Call on a child to provide the correct answer.

Then **say:** *Yes,* **They are animals** *tells how the underlined words are the same.* **Cat, bird, and dog are all animals.** *You should have filled in the answer circle by* **They are animals.** *If you did not fill in the correct answer circle, erase your mark and fill in the answer circle by* **They are animals.**

Harcourt • Reading and Language Skills Assessment

Make sure that children have filled in the correct answer circle. Provide help for children who have difficulty.

Then **say**: *Now I want you to read some more questions that have underlined words in them. First, read each question. Then read the sentences under the question and choose the sentence that tells how the underlined words are the same. Fill in the answer circle by the sentence you choose. Keep working until you come to the word "Stop!" When you come to the word Stop, put your pencils down. Sit quietly until everyone is finished.*

### RESEARCH AND INFORMATION SKILLS: *Alphabetize* (27–30)

**Objective: Alphabetize to the first letter**

**Say**: *Put your finger by the Sample at the top of the page. Find the two rows of words by the Sample. We will read the two rows of words together. Listen while I read the two rows of words aloud.*

*The first row of words says **dog, pin, ant.***

*The second row of words says **ant, dog, pin.***

Then **say**: *Look at the three words in the first row of the Sample: **dog, pin, ant.** Are these words in ABC order? Now look at the three words in the second row of the Sample: **ant, dog, pin.** Are these three words in ABC order? Fill in the answer circle by the row of words that is in ABC order. Pause while children mark their answers.*

Then **say**: *Which row of words is in ABC order—the first row or the second row?* Call on a child to provide the correct answer.

Then **say**: *Yes, the second row of words—**ant, dog, pin**—is in correct ABC order. **Ant** begins with **a**, and **dog** begins*

with **d**. *D comes after **a** in the alphabet. **Pin** begins with **p**. P comes after **d** in the alphabet, so **pin** comes last. You should have filled in the answer circle by the second row of words. If you did not fill in the correct answer circle, erase your mark and fill in the answer circle by the second row of words.*

Make sure that children have filled in the correct answer circle. Provide help for children who have difficulty.

Then **say**: *Now I want you to read some more rows of words by yourself. Read each row of words. Then fill in the answer circle by the row that has the words in ABC order. Keep working until you come to the word "Stop!" When you come to the word Stop, put your pencils down. Sit quietly until everyone is finished.*

### COMPREHENSION: *Plot, Setting, Character, Details, Sequence* (31–36)

**Objective: Identify and describe the elements of plot, setting, and character in a story as well as the story's beginning and ending; recognize important details in a passage; recognize sequence of events**

**Say**: *Put your finger by the Sample at the top of the page. Find the short story called "Carl Finds a Dog." We will read the story together. Follow along while I read the story aloud.*

*Carl saw a little dog in the yard.*

*He called to the dog, and the dog came.*

*The dog looked happy to see Carl.*

*Carl petted the dog and gave him some water.*

Then **say**: *Now find the question under the Sample story. Follow along while I read the question aloud. **What happens*** at the beginning of this story? *Carl petted the dog? Carl gave the dog water? Carl saw a dog in the yard?* Call on a child to provide the correct answer.

Then **say**: *Yes, at the beginning of the story,* **Carl saw a dog in the yard.** *Fill in the answer circle by* **Carl saw a dog in the yard.**

Make sure that children have filled in the correct answer circle. Provide help for children who have difficulty.

Then **say**: *Now I want you to read a longer story and answer the questions about the story by yourself. Keep working until you come to the word "Stop." When you come to the word Stop, put your pencils down. Sit quietly until everyone is finished.*

### COMPREHENSION: Main Idea (Items 37–38)

### Objective: Recognize main idea in a passage

**Say**: *Put your finger by the Sample at the top of the page. Find the short story called "Going to School." We will read the story together. Follow along while I read the story aloud.*

> **Rose likes school.**
>
> **She has a lot of friends there.**
>
> **She reads books at school, and she plays games.**
>
> **She learns so much.**

Then **say**: *Now find the question under the Sample story. Follow along while I read the question aloud. What is this story mostly about? Rose likes school? Rose reads books at school? Rose plays games?* Call on a child to provide the correct answer.

Then **say**: *Yes, this story is mostly about* **Rose likes school.** *Fill in the answer circle by* **Rose likes school.**

Make sure that children have filled in the correct answer circle. Provide help for children who have difficulty.

Then **say**: *Now I want you to read two more stories and answer the questions by yourself. Keep working until you come to the word "Stop."*

### LANGUAGE: Nouns (Items 39–40)

### Objective: Recognize nouns

**Say**: *Put your finger by the Sample. Find the sentence with some words under it. Listen while I read the sentence to you.*

> **He will pick up the rock.**

*Find the words under the sentence. Fill in the answer circle by the noun that names a person, a place, an animal, or a thing.* Pause while children mark their answers.

Then **say**: *Which word names a noun?* Call on a child to provide the correct answer.

Then **say**: *Yes,* **rock** *is a noun that names a thing. You should have filled in the answer circle by* **rock.** *If you did not fill in the correct answer circle, erase your mark and fill in the answer circle by* **rock.**

Make sure that children have filled in the correct answer circle. Provide help for children who have difficulty.

Then **say**: *Now we will read some more sentences together. Follow along while I read each sentence aloud. Then read the answer choices under each sentence and choose the word that names a person, a place, an animal, or a thing.*

Continue the test following the same procedures, reading aloud the sentences for each question. Pause after reading each sentence for children to read the answer choices independently and mark their answers.

**Say:**

39. *The sentence in this row says: **Dick will feed the dog now**. Choose the noun that names a person, a place, an animal, or a thing.*

40. *The sentence in this row says: **Dr. Frank lives by me**. Choose the noun that names a person, a place, an animal, or a thing.*

### LANGUAGE: Pronouns *(Items 41–42)*

**Objective: Recognize pronouns**

In reading aloud the sentences on this subtest, you may use the word *blank* or simply pause where the tested word is missing.

**Say:** *Find the picture of the boy reading a book. Next to the picture is a sentence with a blank in it. The picture will help you figure out which word fits best in the blank. We will read the sentence together. Follow along while I read the sentence aloud.*

_____ **reads a book.**

Then **say:** *Which word fits in the blank to complete the sentence? **He? or It?** Call on a child to provide the correct answer.*

Then **say:** *Yes, **He** completes the sentence. Fill in the answer circle under **He**.*

Make sure that children have filled in the correct answer circle. Provide help for children who have difficulty.

Then **say:** *Now I want you to do some more sentences like this. I will tell you what the picture for each sentence shows. Then you will read the sentences and fill in the answer circle under the word that best completes each sentence.*

Continue the test following the same procedures, telling the children what each picture shows. Pause after identifying each picture for children to read the sentences and mark their

answer choices independently.

**Say:**

41. *The picture shows a woman giving a puppy to a small girl. Read the sentence and choose the word that goes in the blank.*

42. *The picture shows a boy and a girl eating lunch together. Read the sentence and choose the word that goes in the blank.*

### LANGUAGE: Describing words *(Items 43–46)*

**Objective: Recognize adjectives**

**Say:** *Put your finger by the Sample. Find the sentence with a blank in it. We will read the sentence together. Follow along while I read the sentence aloud.*

**I have a _____ coat.**

*There are two words under the sentence. One of the words is a describing word, but the other is **not** a describing word. Which describing word fits in the blank to complete the sentence? **green**? or **hat**? Call on a child to provide the correct answer.*

Then **say:** *Yes, **green** completes the sentence. **I have a green coat**. Fill in the answer circle under **green**.*

Make sure that children have filled in the correct answer circle. Provide help for children who have difficulty.

Then **say:** *Now I want you to read some more sentences by yourself. Then fill in the answer circle under the describing word that best completes each sentence. Keep working until you come to the word "Stop."*

### LANGUAGE: Verbs *(Items 47–48)*

**Objective: Recognize action words**

**Say:** *Put your finger by the Sample. Find the sentence with some words under it.*

Harcourt • Reading and Language Skills Assessment

We will read the sentence together. Follow along while I read the sentence aloud.

**Two ducks quacked.**

Then **say:** *Which word is the verb from the sentence? Two? ducks? quacked? Call on a child to provide the correct answer.*

Then **say:** *Yes, **quacked** is the verb. Fill in the answer circle by **quacked.***

Make sure that children have filled in the correct answer circle. Provide help for children who have difficulty.

Then **say:** *Now I want you to read two more sentences and answer the questions by yourself. Fill in the answer circle by the verb from each sentence. The verb might tell about now, or it might tell about the past. Keep working until you come to the word "Stop."*

Harcourt • Reading and Language Skills Assessment

# Scoring and Interpreting the Assessments

The *Mid-Year and End-of-Year Reading Skills Assessments* can be scored by using the answer keys found in the Appendix. Follow these steps:

1. Turn to the appropriate answer key in the Appendix.
2. Compare the student's responses, item by item, to the answer key and put a check mark next to each item that is correctly answered.
3. Count the number of correct responses for each skill category and write that number on the "Pupil Score" line on the cover of the assessment booklet. Add the Pupil Scores for each skill category to obtain the student's Total Score.
4. Next, determine if the child met the criterion for Total Score. The criterion score can be found on the cover page of the assessment booklet. Use the "Interpreting Performance" chart found in this section of the Teacher's Edition booklet to interpret the student's score.
5. If a child does not reach the overall criterion on the total test, you may evaluate the child's performance on particular skill categories. Look at each skill category and determine if the child met the criterion for that skill category. Then determine the child's strengths and weaknesses for particular skill categories. Write comments in the space provided.

There are 50 items on the *Mid-Year Reading and Language Skills Assessment* and 48 items on the *End-of-Year Reading and Language Skills Assessment*. For each item, a correct answer should be given 1 point, and an incorrect or missing answer should be given 0 points. Thus, a perfect score on *Mid-Year Reading and Language Assessment* would be 50, and a perfect score on the *End-of-Year Reading and Language Assessment* would be 48. Use the following performance chart to interpret score ranges.

## Interpreting Performance on the
## *Mid-Year* and *End-of-Year Reading Skills Assessments*

| Total Score | Interpretation | Teaching Suggestions |
|---|---|---|
| **Mid-Year: 38–50** <br> **End-of-Year: 35–48** | Average to excellent understanding and use of the major reading and language skills | Children scoring at the high end of this range exceed the criterion and should have no difficulty moving forward to the next level of the program. <br><br> Children scoring at the low end of this range meet the criterion and are performing at an acceptable level. |
| **Mid-Year: 0–37** <br> **End-of-Year: 0–34** | Fair to limited understanding and use of the major reading and language skills | Children scoring at the high end of this range are performing slightly below the criterion and may need extra help before or after moving to the next level of the program. Note whether performance varied across the skill categories tested. Examine other samples of the children's work and/or administer some of the individual assessments (e.g., Phonics Inventory, Oral Reading Fluency Assessment) to confirm their progress and pinpoint instructional needs. <br><br> Children scoring at the low end of this range do not meet criterion and should have their performance verified through other measures such as some of the individual assessments available in this program, or daily work samples. Identify what specific instructional needs must be met by reviewing the student's performance on each skill category. |

Harcourt • Reading and Language Skills Assessment

A child who does not reach the criterion level may not do so for a variety of reasons. Use the questions that follow to better understand why a child may not have reached the criterion.

- *Has the child completed all parts of the program being tested on the assessment?*

    If not, the results may not be valid since the *Mid-Year Reading and Language Skills Assessment* evaluates all the major skills taught in the first three books at this grade level, and the *End-of-Year Reading and Language Skills Assessment* evaluates the major skills taught in all five books at this grade level. It would be unfair to expect a child to demonstrate mastery of skills for which he or she has not received instruction.

- *Was the child having a bad day when he or she took the assessment??*

    Children can experience social or emotional problems that may affect concentration and influence performance. Sometimes a problem at home or a conflict on the school playground carries over into the classroom and interferes with performance. Recall any unusual behavior you observed before or during the testing, or confer with the child to identify any factors that may have adversely affected performance. If the child's limited performance can be attributed to extraneous problems, readminister the assessment under better conditions or discard the results.

- *Does the child perform differently on group tests than on individual tests?*

    Student performance can fluctuate depending on the context and mode of the assessment. Some children perform better in a one-on-one setting that fosters individual attention than they do in a group setting that is less personal. Others are more successful reading orally than reading silently. Likewise, some children feel more comfortable answering open-ended questions orally than they do answering multiple-choice questions on a paper-and-pencil test.

- *Does the child perform differently on tests than on daily activities?*

    Compare the child's performance on the mid-year and the end-of-year assessment with his or her performance on other formal types of assessment, such as theme tests and standardized tests. Also note how the child's performance compares with his or her performance on informal types of assessment, such as portfolios, reading logs, and anecdotal observation records. If the results are similar, it would suggest that the mid-year and the end-of-year results are valid and accurately represent the child's performance. If the results are not consistent, explore alternative explanations.

To resolve conflicts regarding the child's performance, you may want to collect additional evidence. For example, you may want to administer some of the individual assessments available with this program (e.g., Phonemic Awareness Inventory, Phonics Inventory, Oral Reading Fluency Assessment).

As with all assessments, it is important not to place too much faith in a single test. The *Mid-Year* and *End-of-Year Reading and Language Skills Assessments* are just one observation of a child's reading behavior. They should be combined with other evidence of a child's progress, such as the teacher's daily observations, the child's work samples, and individual reading conferences. The sum of all this information, combined with test scores, is more reliable and valid than any single piece of information.

# Appendix

• • • • • • • • • • • • • • • • • • • • • • • • • • • • • • • • • • • • • • • • • • • •

**Answer Keys**

Answer Keys for *Reading and Language Skills Assessments:*
*Pretest* and *Posttests*

Answer Keys for *Mid-Year* and *End-of-Year Reading and Language Skills Assessments*

**Assessment Booklets**

*Guess Who*/Book 1-1: Pretest

*Guess Who*/Book 1-1: Posttest

*Catch a Dream*/Book 1-2: Pretest

*Catch a Dream*/Book 1-2: Posttest

*Here and There*/Book 1-3: Pretest

*Here and There*/Book 1-3: Posttest

*Mid-Year Reading and Language Skills Assessment Booklet*

*Time Together*/Book 1-4: Pretest

*Time Together*/Book 1-4: Posttest

*Gather Around*/Book 1-5: Pretest

*Gather Around/* Book 1-5: Posttest

*End-of-Year Reading and Language Skills Assessment Booklet*

# Answer Keys for *Reading and Language Skills Assessments:* Posttests and Posttests
## *Guess Who/*Book 1-1

| PRETEST | POSTTEST |
|---|---|
| **DECODING**<br>**Vowels: Phonemes**<br>1. cat<br>2. cap<br>3. sit<br>4. rip<br>5. stop<br>6. hop | **DECODING**<br>**Vowels: Phonemes**<br>1. bat<br>2. fan<br>3. dig<br>4. pin<br>5. rock<br>6. top |
| **Vowels: Decodable Words**<br>7. sip<br>8. hill<br>9. sack<br>10. man<br>11. top<br>12. lock | **Vowels: Decodable Words**<br>7. lip<br>8. sit<br>9. hat<br>10. map<br>11. fox<br>12. sock |
| **Digraphs: Sound-Letter Relationships**<br>13. chick<br>14. kick<br>15. lock<br>16. tack | **Digraphs: Sound-Letter Relationships**<br>13. rock<br>14. sock<br>15. tack<br>16. chick |
| **COMPREHENSION:**<br>**Sequence**<br>17. She put ice cream in two bowls.<br>18. They sat down to eat their snack.<br>19. a kangaroo<br>20. a tiger | **COMPREHENSION:**<br>**Sequence**<br>17. She put on Mom's hat.<br>18. She laughed at how she looked.<br>19. He dug up some worms.<br>20. He and Dad went fishing. |
| **LANGUAGE**<br>21. Yes<br>22. No<br>23. period<br>24. question mark<br>25. My mom<br>26. The lamp | **LANGUAGE**<br>21. Yes<br>22. No<br>23. period<br>24. question mark<br>25. You<br>26. My cat |

Harcourt • Reading and Language Skills Assessment

| PRETEST | POSTTEST |
|---|---|
| **DECODING**<br>**Vowels: Phonemes**<br>1. bed     4. run<br>2. desk    5. fork<br>3. bus     6. store | **DECODING:**<br>**Vowels: Phonemes**<br>1. sled    4. nut<br>2. nest    5. storm<br>3. gum     6. snore |
| **Vowels: Decodable Words**<br>7. mess     10. stuck<br>8. ten      11. horn<br>9. nut      12. snore | **Vowels:**<br>**Decodable Words**<br>7. leg      10. rug<br>8. bell     11. thorn<br>9. duck    12. fort |
| **Initial Blends:**<br>**Sound-Letter Relationships**<br>13. frog     21. dress<br>14. store    22. spill<br>15. press    23. smell<br>16. sled     24. skip<br>17. grass    25. swim<br>18. snail    26. brush<br>19. crab     27. tree<br>20. scoop | **Initial Blends: Sound-Letter**<br>**Relationships**<br>13. fruit     21. drum<br>14. stamp   22. spoon<br>15. pretzel   23. smile<br>16. slip     24. skunk<br>17. grapes   25. swing<br>18. snail     26. brick<br>19. crow    27. train<br>20. scared |
| **Digraphs: Sound-Letter**<br>**Relationships**<br>28. ship     30. bath<br>29. think    31. fish | **Digraphs: Sound-Letter**<br>**Relationships**<br>28. sheep    30. moth<br>29. thorn    31. dish |
| **COMPREHENSION:**<br>**Details**<br>32. Dad      35. ride it to<br>33. a dress        school<br>34. a bike | **COMPREHENSION:**<br>**Details**<br>32. Carl     34. roses<br>33. juice    35. four |
| **LANGUAGE**<br>36. naming part   39. boy<br>37. naming part   40. pond<br>38. telling part    41. doll | **LANGUAGE**<br>36. naming part   39. girl<br>37. naming part   40. pen<br>38. telling part    41. truck |

## Answer Keys for *Reading and Language Skills Assessments:* Pretests and Posttests

### *Here and There/Book 1-3*

| PRETEST | POSTTEST |
|---|---|
| **DECODING**<br>**Vowels: Phonemes**<br>1. boat    4. cart<br>2. crow    5. skirt<br>3. jar    6. purse | **DECODING:**<br>**Vowels: Phonemes**<br>1. goat    4. star<br>2. snow    5. girl<br>3. harp    6. shirt |
| **Vowels: Decodable Words**<br>7. coat    10. card<br>8. crow    11. bird<br>9. barn    12. third | **Vowels:**<br>**Decodable Words**<br>7. road    10. cart<br>8. throw    11. first<br>9. harp    12. girl |
| **Initial Blends:**<br>**Sound-Letter Relationships**<br>13. blow    19. chick<br>14. class    20. quack<br>15. flag    21. whistle<br>16. glass    22. queen<br>17. plant    23. wheat<br>18. slip    24. lunch | **Initial Blends: Sound-Letter**<br>**Relationships**<br>13. block    19. chest<br>14. clap    20. quarter<br>15. fly    21. whip<br>16. glue    22. question<br>17. plant    23. wheel<br>18. sled    24. catch |
| **Inflections**<br>25. sinking    27. calling<br>26. looked    28. packs | **Inflections**<br>25. thinking    27. barking<br>26. hunted    28. cracks |
| **COMPREHENSION:**<br>**Setting and Character**<br>29. on a farm    32. at Fran's pond<br>30. spring    33. at lunch time<br>31. Ann    34. an ant | **COMPREHENSION:**<br>**Setting and Character**<br>29. on a bed    33. in the<br>30. at night    morning<br>31. Meg's cat    34. Sal<br>32. at school |
| **LANGUAGE**<br>35. pig    38. Hill Street<br>36. horse    39. Uncle Ned<br>37. Mr. Smith    40. Sun Park | **LANGUAGE**<br>35. fish    38. Park Street<br>36. chickens    39. Mrs. Conn<br>37. Dr. Mills    40. Pebble Pond |

Harcourt • Reading and Language Skills Assessment

| PRETEST | POSTTEST |
|---|---|
| **DECODING**<br>**Vowels: Decodable Words**<br>1. sheep<br>2. read<br>3. spike<br>4. bike<br>5. skate<br>6. lake<br>7. dome<br>8. mole | **DECODING:**<br>**Vowels: Decodable Words**<br>1. queen<br>2. seal<br>3. line<br>4. ride<br>5. lake<br>6. bake<br>7. note<br>8. mole |
| **Contractions**<br>9. She will<br>10. Who is<br>11. Do not<br>12. He is | **Contractions**<br>9. can not<br>10. Do not<br>11. He is<br>12. She will |
| **VOCABULARY:**<br>**Classify/Categorize**<br>13. They are drinks.<br>14. They have wheels.<br>15. They are foods to eat.<br>16. They are things to wear. | **VOCABULARY:**<br>**Classify/Categorize**<br>13. They are foods.<br>14. They are insects.<br>15. They have water.<br>16. They are plants. |
| **RESEARCH AND**<br>**INFORMATION SKILLS:**<br>**Alphabetize**<br>17. egg, lock, nose<br>18. rose, truck, wig<br>19. cream, fire, king<br>20. oak, silk, vase | **RESEARCH AND**<br>**INFORMATION SKILLS:**<br>**Alphabetize**<br>17. grass, hog, mice<br>18. inch, step, trap<br>19. Carl, Dave, Jan<br>20. pet, ranch, wig |
| **LANGUAGE**<br>21. it<br>22. She<br>23. I<br>24. They<br>25. three<br>26. red<br>27. hot<br>28. happy | **LANGUAGE**<br>21. They<br>22. I<br>23. He<br>24. It<br>25. two<br>26. blue<br>27. sweet<br>28. sad |

| PRETEST | POSTTEST |
|---|---|
| **DECODING:** | **DECODING:** |
| **Vowels: Decodable Words** | **Vowels: Decodable Words** |
| 1. nail | 1. paint |
| 2. hay | 2. tray |
| 3. light | 3. might |
| 4. flight | 4. light |
| 5. mule | 5. cube |
| 6. prune | 6. tube |
| **Inflections** | **Inflections** |
| 7. running | 7. clapping |
| 8. stopped | 8. slipped |
| 9. riding | 9. hiding |
| 10. baked | 10. lined |
| **Contractions** | **Contractions** |
| 11. We have | 11. We are |
| 12. I would | 12. I would |
| 13. She would | 13. He would |
| 14. You are | 14. They have |
| **COMPREHENSION:** | **COMPREHENSION:** |
| **Plot** | **Plot** |
| 15. The hens on a farm are upset. | 15. Tip wants to be big and strong. |
| 16. a fox | 16. Tom Cat |
| 17. The fox comes back late at night. | 17. Tip gets big and strong. |
| 18. The fox leaves and does not come back. | 18. Tom Cat runs away when Tip barks. |
| **COMPREHENSION:** | **COMPREHENSION:** |
| **Main Idea** | **Main Idea** |
| 19. Bess made a cake. | 19. Dad helped Rob make a kite. |
| 20. Dad fixed the bike tire. | 20. Tonya and Kim made cards for Mom. |
| 21. Les and Jen planted seeds. | 21. Grandpa and I like to do things together. |
| 22. Jed helped his mom wash the dishes. | 22. I help at home in many ways. |
| **LANGUAGE** | **LANGUAGE** |
| 23. plays | 23. chases |
| 24. smiled | 24. played |
| 25. drives | 25. ripped |
| 26. are | 26. is |
| 27. fills | 27. throws |
| 28. jumped | 28. hiked |

Harcourt • Reading and Language Skills Assessment

**DECODING**
1. sit
2. cap
3. hop
4. run
5. bed
6. boat
7. skirt
8. fork
9. jar
10. hill
11. man
12. coat
13. top
14. mess
15. nut
16. horn
17. barn
18. bird
19. smell
20. store
21. trash
22. crab
23. blow
24. glass
25. quack
26. wheat
27. lock

28. fish
29. bath
30. lunch
31. growing
32. spilled
33. reading
34. helps

**COMPREHENSION**
35. in the morning
36. get up
37. get dressed
38. his friends
39. at bed time
40. a snack
41. Ann
42. They sat down to eat their snack.

**LANGUAGE**
43. Yes
44. No
45. period
46. question mark
47. naming part
48. telling part
49. mouse
50. West Street

## Answer Key
### *End-of-Year Reading* and *Language Skills Assessment*

**DECODING**
1. sheep
2. read
3. skate
4. nail
5. hay
6. light
7. dome
8. bike
9. prune
10. crow
11. barn
12. third
13. grinning
14. rubbed
15. coming
16. moved
17. He will
18. Do not
19. She is
20. You have
21. She would
22. You are

**VOCABULARY**
23. They are foods.
24. They are things in the sky.
25. They live in the water.
26. They are things to wear.

**RESEARCH AND INFORMATION SKILLS**
27. fox, leg, nest
28. race, tub, whistle
29. cage, fight, jar
30. ostrich, step, vest

**COMPREHENSION**
31. see animals
32. to the country
33. Mom
34. some deer
35. a horse
36. Pete runs to tell Dad what they saw.
37. There are many kinds of fish.
38. You should take good care of a puppy.

**LANGUAGE**
39. dog
40. Dr. Frank
41. She
42. They
43. six
44. cold
45. rainy
46. hungry
47. ran
48. are

Harcourt • Reading and Language Skills Assessment

# Student Record Form
## *Reading and Language Skills Assessment*
### *Trophies*
### Grade 1

**Name** _____ **Grade** _____

**Teacher** _____

| | CRITERION SCORE | PUPIL SCORE | COMMENTS |
|---|---|---|---|
| ***Guess Who*/Book 1-1** | | | |
| Vowels: Phonemes (/a/*a*, /i/*i*; /o/*o*) | 4/6 | /6 | _____ |
| Vowels: Decodable Words | 4/6 | /6 | _____ |
| Digraphs: Sound-Letter Relationships (/k/*ck*) | 3/4 | /4 | _____ |
| Sequence | 3/4 | /4 | _____ |
| Language | 4/6 | /6 | _____ |
| ***Catch a Dream*/Book 1-2** | | | |
| Vowels: Phonemes (/e/*e*; /u/*u*, /ôr/*or, ore*) | 4/6 | /6 | _____ |
| Vowels: Decodable Words | 4/6 | /6 | _____ |
| Initial Blends: Sound-Letter Relationships (blends with *r* and *s*) | 11/15 | /15 | _____ |
| Digraphs: Sound-Letter Relationships (/th/*th*; /sh/*sh*) | 3/4 | /4 | _____ |
| Details | 3/4 | /4 | _____ |
| Language | 4/6 | /6 | _____ |
| ***Here and There*/Book 1-3** | | | |
| Vowels: Phonemes (/ō/*ow, oa*; /är/*ar*; /ûr/*er, ir, ur*) | 4/6 | /6 | _____ |
| Vowels: Decodable Words | 4/6 | /6 | _____ |
| Initial Blends: Sound-Letter Relationships (blends with *l*) | 4/6 | /6 | _____ |
| Digraphs: Sound-Letter Relationships (/ch/*ch, tch*; /kw/*qu*; /hw/*wh*) | 4/6 | /6 | _____ |
| Inflections (*-s, -ed, -ing*) | 3/4 | /4 | _____ |
| Setting and Character | 4/6 | /6 | _____ |
| Language | 4/6 | /6 | _____ |

Name _____ Grade _____

Teacher _____

| | CRITERION SCORE | PUPIL SCORE | COMMENTS |
|---|---|---|---|
| ***Time Together*/Book 1-4** | | | |
| Vowels: Decodable Words (/ē/e, ee, ea; /ā/a-e; /ī/i-e; /ō/o-e) | 6/8 | /8 | _____ |
| Word Structure: Contractions ('s, n't, 'll) | 3/4 | /4 | _____ |
| Classify/Categorize | 3/4 | /4 | _____ |
| Alphabetize | 3/4 | /4 | _____ |
| Language | 6/8 | /8 | _____ |
| | | | |
| ***Gather Around*/Book 1-5** | | | |
| Vowels: Decodable Words (/ī/igh; /ā/ai, ay; /o͞o/u-e) | 4/6 | /6 | _____ |
| Inflections (-ed, -ing) | 3/4 | /4 | _____ |
| Contractions ('ve, 'd, 're) | 3/4 | /4 | _____ |
| Plot | 3/4 | /4 | _____ |
| Main Idea | 3/4 | /4 | _____ |
| Language | 4/6 | /6 | _____ |

Harcourt • Reading and Language Skills Assessment

# ·TROPHIES·

# Reading and Language Skills
# Assessment Pretest

## Guess Who/Book 1-1

Name _____ Date _____

| SKILL AREA | Criterion Score | Pupil Score | Pupil Strength |
|---|---|---|---|
| **DECODING** | | | |
| Short Vowels | | | |
| /a/a; /i/i; /o/o | | | |
| Phonemes | 4/6 | | |
| Decodable Words | 4/6 | _____ | _____ |
| Digraphs | | | |
| /k/ck | | | |
| Sound-Letter Relationships | 3/4 | _____ | _____ |
| | | | |
| **COMPREHENSION** | | | |
| Sequence | 3/4 | _____ | _____ |
| | | | |
| **LANGUAGE** | 4/6 | _____ | _____ |
| Sentences | | | |
| Word Order | | | |
| Telling Sentences | | | |
| Asking Sentences | | | |
| Naming Parts of Sentences | | | |
| | | | |
| **TOTAL SCORE** | 18/26 | _____ | _____ |

Were accommodations made in administering this test?  ☐ Yes  ☐ No

Type of accommodations: _____

_____

Printed in the United States of America

ISBN 0-15-332155-5

8 9 10   170   10 09 08 07 06 05 04

**DECODING:** Vowels: Phonemes

**Sample**

**1.**

**2.**

**3.**

GO ON ▶

Harcourt • Reading and Language Skills Assessment

**DECODING:** Vowels: Phonemes (continued)

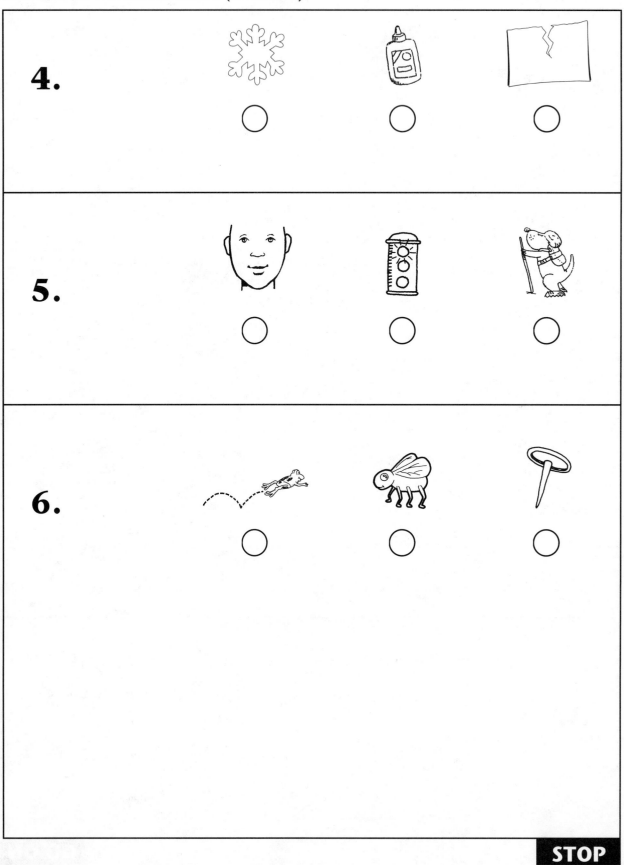

**4.**

○   ○   ○

**5.**

○   ○   ○

**6.**

○   ○   ○

**STOP**

**Score** _____       *Guess Who* / Book 1-1

**DECODING:** Vowels: Decodable Words

# Sample

dad     ○

dip     ○

dim     ○

**7.**

Sam     ○

sip     ○

sap     ○

**8.**

ham     ○

hat     ○

hill     ○

**9.**

sill     ○

sack     ○

sit     ○

**GO ON**

**DECODING:** Vowels: Decodable Words (continued)

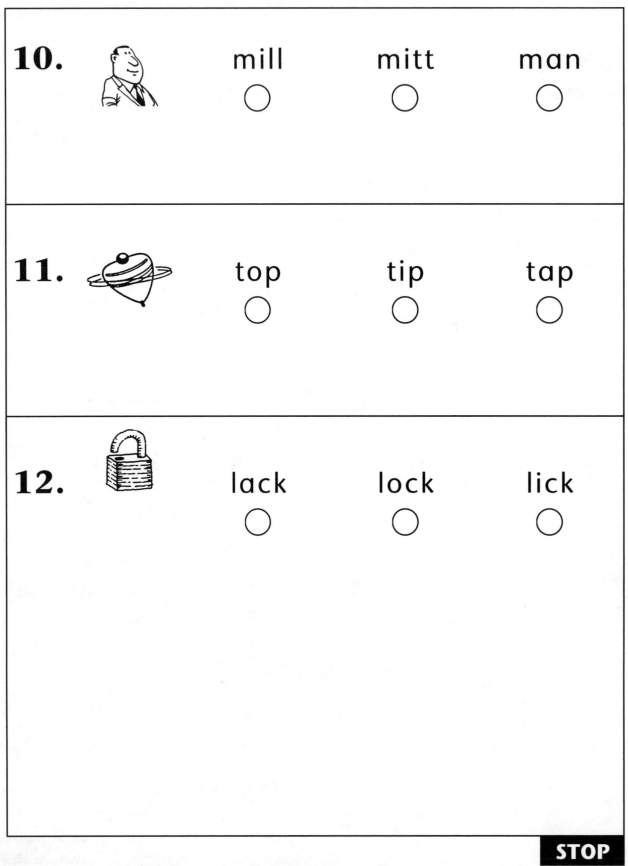

**10.**  mill $\bigcirc$    mitt $\bigcirc$    man $\bigcirc$

**11.**  top $\bigcirc$    tip $\bigcirc$    tap $\bigcirc$

**12.**  lack $\bigcirc$    lock $\bigcirc$    lick $\bigcirc$

**STOP**

Harcourt • Reading and Language Skills Assessment

**DECODING:** Digraphs: Sound-Letter Relationships

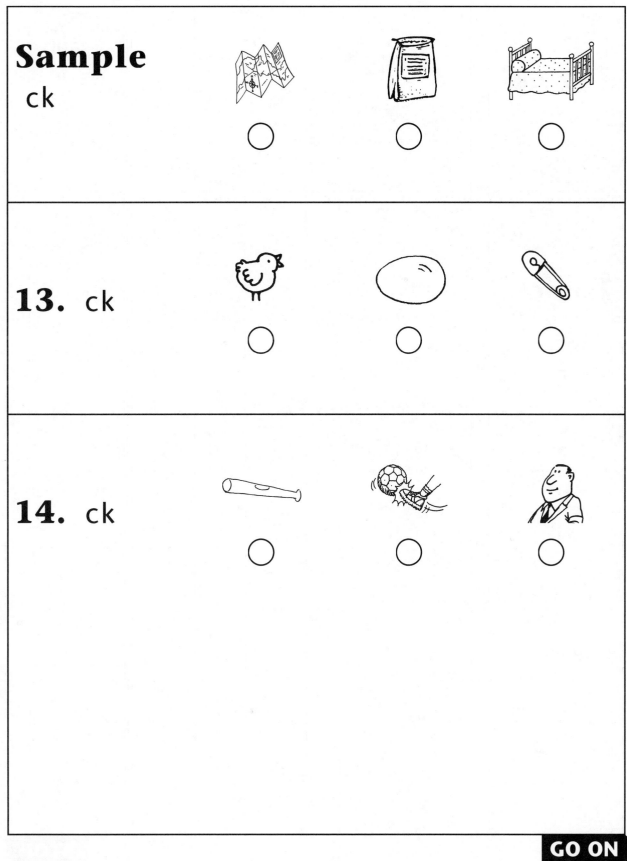

**Sample**

ck

○   ○   ○

**13.** ck

○   ○   ○

**14.** ck

○   ○   ○

**GO ON**

**DECODING:** Digraphs: Sound-Letter Relationships (continued)

**15.** ck

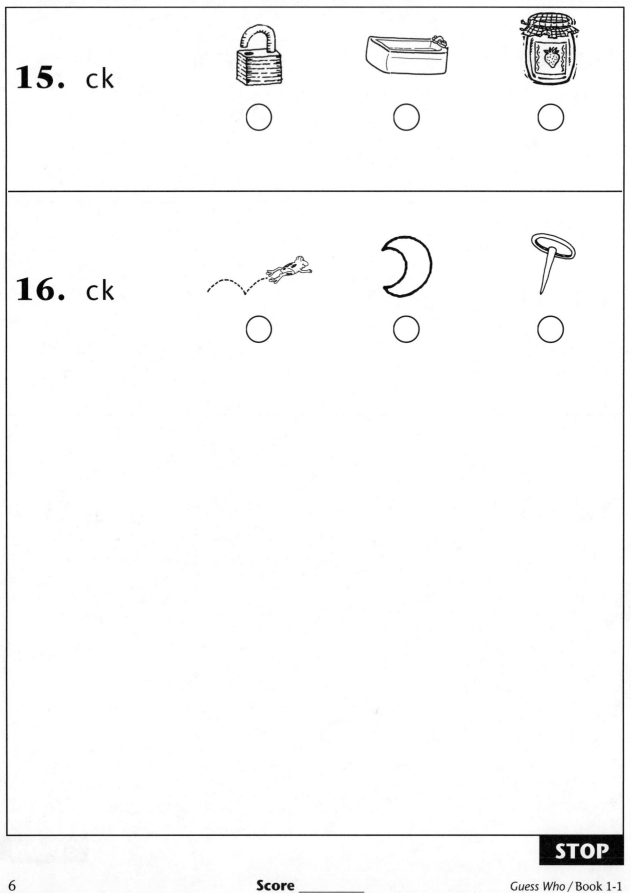

○        ○        ○

**16.** ck

○        ○        ○

**STOP**

**COMPREHENSION:** Sequence

## Sample

# Growing a Plant

Here is how to grow a plant.
Put the plant in the sun.
Give the plant a drink every day.
Watch the plant grow.

What should you do **first**?
- ○ Watch the plant grow.
- ○ Put the plant in the sun.
- ○ Give the plant a drink.

**GO ON**

**COMPREHENSION:** Sequence (continued)

# Cam Makes a Snack

Cam helped her friend make a snack. First, her friend put ice cream in two bowls.

Then, Cam put nuts on the ice cream. Last, Cam and her friend sat down to eat their snack.

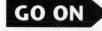

Harcourt • Reading and Language Skills Assessment

**COMPREHENSION:** Sequence (continued)

**17.** What did the friend do **first**?

○ She put ice cream in two bowls.

○ She put nuts on the ice cream.

○ She had a drink.

**18.** What did Cam and her friend do **last**?

○ They put nuts on the ice cream.

○ They put ice cream in two bowls.

○ They sat down to eat their snack.

# Beth and Dan

Beth and Dan were reading a book.
First, they read about a kangaroo.
Next, they read about a hippo.
Last, they read about a tiger.
Beth and Dan had fun reading.

**COMPREHENSION:** Sequence (continued)

**19.** What did Beth and Dan read about **first**?

  ⃝  a hippo

  ⃝  a kangaroo

  ⃝  a tiger

**20.** What did Beth and Dan read about **last**?

  ⃝  a hippo

  ⃝  a kangaroo

  ⃝  a tiger

**STOP**

**LANGUAGE**

# Sample 1

my cat? Where is

Yes          No

○            ○

**21.** I see a red apple.

Yes          No

○            ○

**22.** big surprise. Look at my

Yes          No

○            ○

**GO ON**

**LANGUAGE** (continued)

# Sample 2

Will you come now

.          ?

○          ○

---

**23.** The jam is good

.          ?

○          ○

---

**24.** Where is my snack

.          ?

○          ○

**GO ON** ➤

## Sample 3

I went with him.

   I       went with him

   ◯        ◯

**25.** My mom is here.

   My mom   is here

   ◯      ◯

**26.** The lamp is lit.

   The lamp   is lit

   ◯      ◯

**STOP**

Harcourt • Reading and Language Skills Assessment

# Guess Who/Book 1-1

## Reading and Language Skills Assessment

**Harcourt**

Orlando  Boston  Dallas  Chicago  San Diego

Part No. 9997-37692-7

ISBN 0-15-332155-5  (Package of 12)

1-1

# TROPHIES

# Reading and Language Skills Assessment Posttest

## Guess Who/Book 1-1

Name _____ Date _____

| SKILL AREA | Criterion Score | Pupil Score | Pupil Strength |
|---|---|---|---|
| **DECODING** | | | |
| Short vowels /a/a; /i/i; /o/o | | | |
| Phonemes | 4/6 | _____ | _____ |
| Decodable Words | 4/6 | _____ | _____ |
| Digraphs /k/ck | | | |
| Sound-Letter Relationships | 3/4 | _____ | _____ |
| | | | |
| **COMPREHENSION** | | | |
| Sequence | 3/4 | _____ | _____ |
| | | | |
| **LANGUAGE** | 4/6 | _____ | _____ |
| Sequence | | | |
| Word Order | | | |
| Telling Sentences | | | |
| Asking Sentences | | | |
| Naming Parts of Sentences | | | |
| | | | |
| **TOTAL SCORE** | 18/26 | _____ | _____ |

Were accommodations made in administering this test? ☐ Yes ☐ No

Type of accommodations: _____

_____

**DECODING:** Vowels: Phonemes

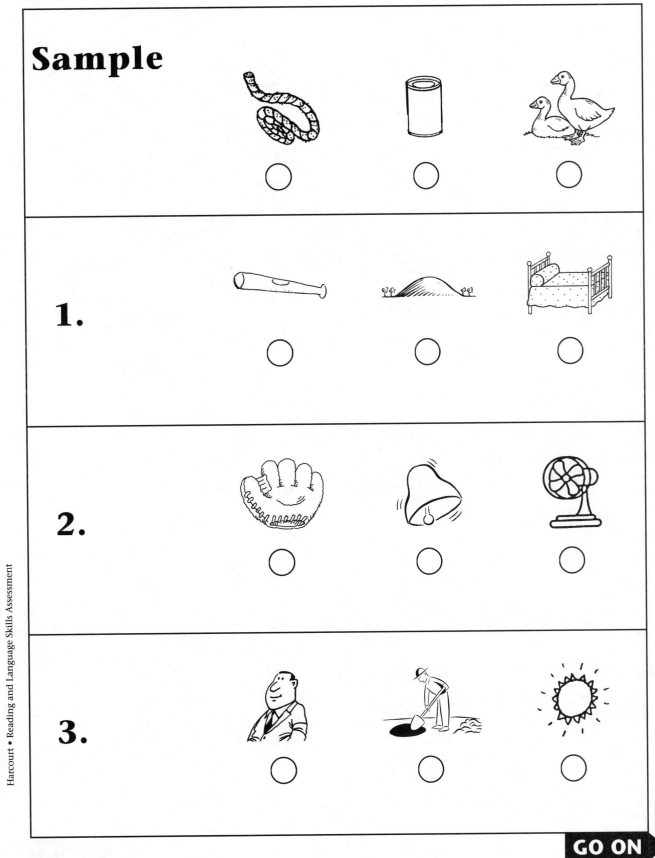

**Sample**

**1.**

**2.**

**3.**

**GO ON**

**DECODING:** Vowels: Phonemes (continued)

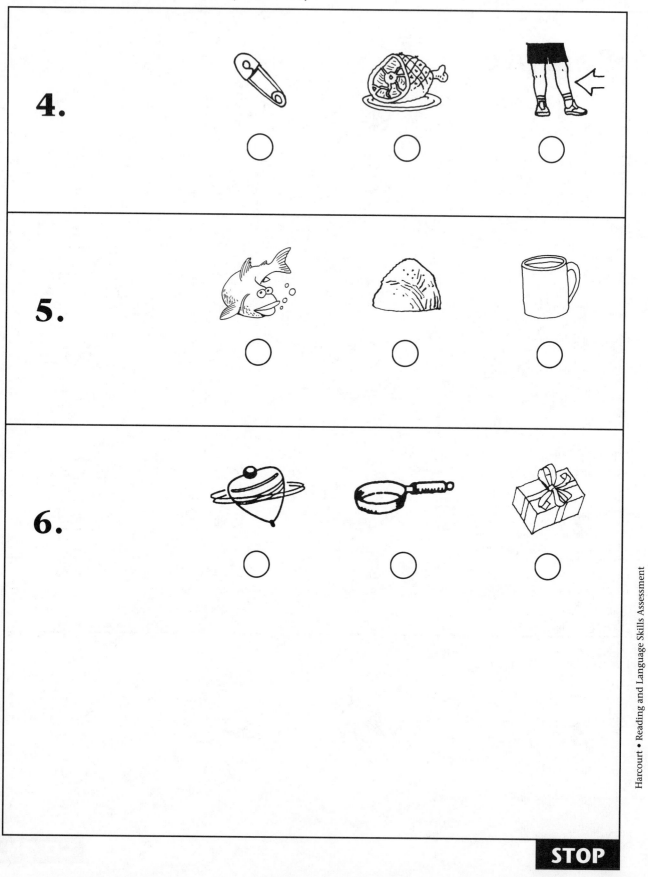

**4.**

**5.**

**6.**

**STOP**

**Score** _____

Harcourt • Reading and Language Skills Assessment

**DECODING:** Vowels: Decodable Words

# Sample

dad ⭕    dip ⭕    dim ⭕

**7.** lap ⭕    lip ⭕    log ⭕

**8.** sit ⭕    sad ⭕    sat ⭕

**9.** hot ⭕    him ⭕    hat ⭕

**GO ON ▶**

**DECODING:** Vowels: Decodable Words (continued)

**10.**    mitt     map     mop
     ◯      ◯      ◯

**11.**    fox     fat     fig
     ◯      ◯      ◯

**12.**    sack     sick     sock
     ◯      ◯      ◯

**STOP**

**Score** _____

*Guess Who / Book 1-1*

Harcourt • Reading and Language Skills Assessment

**DECODING:** Digraphs: Sound-Letter Relationships

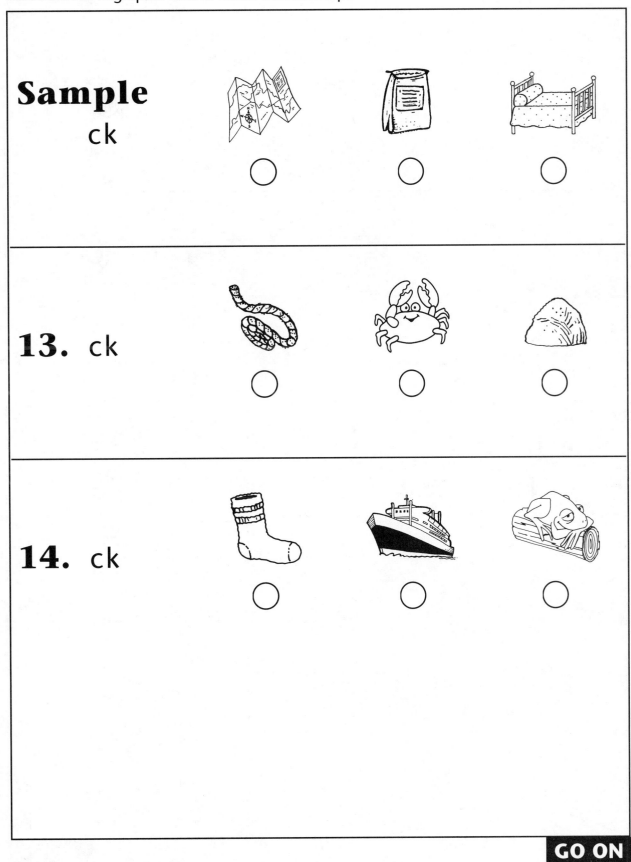

**Sample**
ck
○          ○          ○

**13.** ck
○          ○          ○

**14.** ck
○          ○          ○

**GO ON** ▶

**DECODING:** Digraphs: Sound-Letter Relationships (continued)

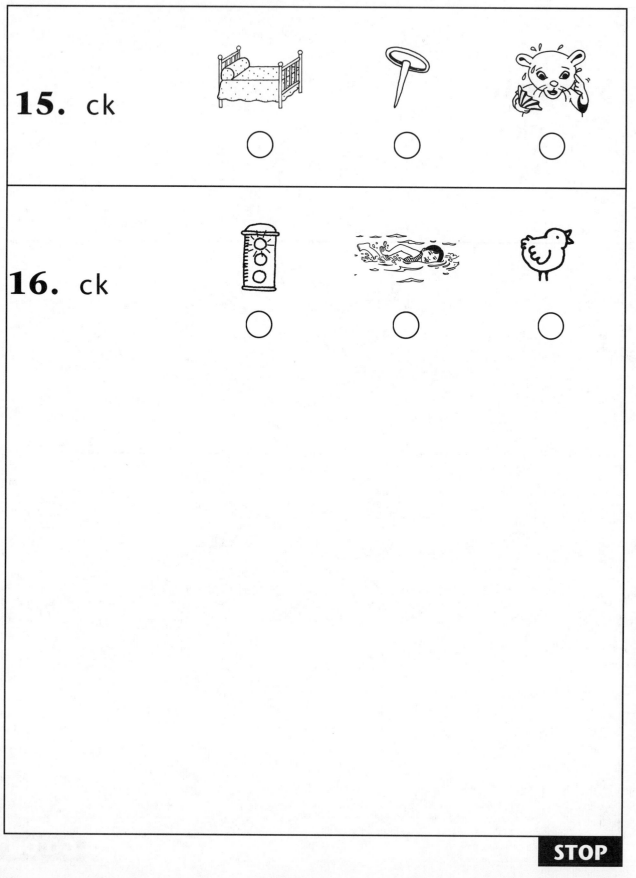

**15.** ck

⭕    ⭕    ⭕

**16.** ck

⭕    ⭕    ⭕

**Score** _____       *Guess Who* / Book 1-1

Harcourt • Reading and Language Skills Assessment

**COMPREHENSION:** Sequence

## Sample

### Growing a Plant

Here is how to grow a plant.
Put the plant in the sun.
Give the plant a drink every day.
Watch the plant grow.

What should you do **first**?

○  Watch the plant grow.

○  Put the plant in the sun.

○  Give the plant a drink.

**GO ON**

**COMPREHENSION:** Sequence (continued)

# Dress Up

First, Liz put on Mom's hat.
Then, she put on Mom's coat.
The hat and coat were too big!
Last, Liz laughed at how she
looked.

Harcourt • Reading and Language Skills Assessment

**COMPREHENSION:** Sequence (continued)

**17.** What did Liz do **first**?

○   She put on Mom's coat.

○   She put on Mom's hat.

○   She laughed at how she looked.

**18.** What did Liz do **last**?

○   She put on Mom's coat.

○   She put on Mom's hat.

○   She laughed at how she looked.

**GO ON**

**COMPREHENSION:** Sequence (continued)

# Going Fishing

Dad and Jake wanted to go fishing.
First, Jake dug up some worms.
Next, he put the worms in a can.
He showed the can of worms to Dad.
Last, Jake and Dad went fishing.

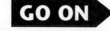

**COMPREHENSION:** Sequence (continued)

**19.** What did Jake do **first**?

○ He put worms in a can.

○ He went fishing with Dad.

○ He dug up some worms.

**20.** What did Jake do **last**?

○ He put worms in a can.

○ He and Dad went fishing.

○ He showed the can of worms to Dad.

**STOP**

**LANGUAGE**

## Sample 1

my cat? Where is

Yes          No
◯            ◯

---

**21.** Pam said she will come.

Yes          No
◯            ◯

---

**22.** little fish. I see a

Yes          No
◯            ◯

**GO ON** ▶

**LANGUAGE** (continued)

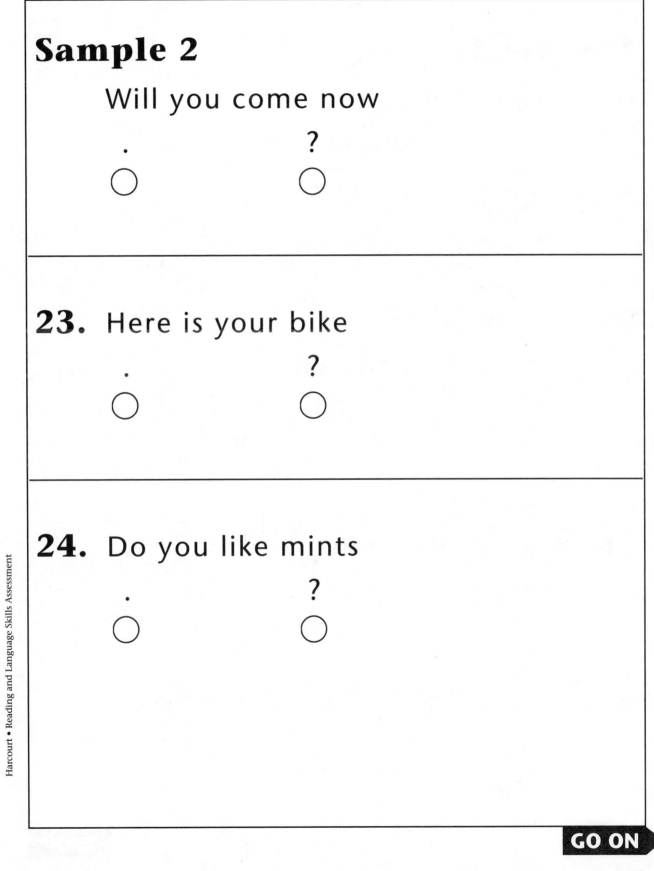

**Sample 2**

Will you come now

.          ?

◯          ◯

**23.** Here is your bike

.          ?

◯          ◯

**24.** Do you like mints

.          ?

◯          ◯

**GO ON**

Harcourt • Reading and Language Skills Assessment

**LANGUAGE** (continued)

## Sample 3

I went with him.

I           went with him

○           ○

**25.** You may see it.

You        may see it

○         ○

**26.** My cat likes milk.

My cat      likes milk

○         ○

**STOP**

Harcourt • Reading and Language Skills Assessment

· TROPHIES ·

# Guess Who/Book 1-1
## Reading and Language Skills Assessment

**Harcourt**

Orlando  Boston  Dallas  Chicago  San Diego

Part No. 9997-37693-5

ISBN 0-15-332155-5  (Package of 12)

1-1

## · T R O P H I E S ·

# Reading and Language Skills Assessment Pretest

## Catch a Dream/Book 1-2

Name _____ Date _____

| SKILL AREA | Criterion Score | Pupil Score | Pupil Strength |
|---|---|---|---|
| **DECODING** | | | |
| Short Vowels /e/e; /u/u | | | |
| R-controlled Vowels /ôr/or, ore | | | |
| Phonemes | 4/6 | _____ | _____ |
| Decodable Words | 4/6 | _____ | _____ |
| Initial Blends with *r* and *s* br, cr, dr, fr, gr, pr, tr sc, sk, sl, sm, sn, sp, st, sw | | | |
| Sound-Letter Relationships | 11/15 | _____ | _____ |
| Digraphs /th/th; /sh/sh | | | |
| Sound-Letter Relationships | 3/4 | _____ | _____ |
| **COMPREHENSION** | | | |
| Details | 3/4 | _____ | _____ |
| **LANGUAGE** | 4/6 | _____ | _____ |
| Naming Parts for Two Telling Parts of Sentences Telling Parts for Two Complete Sentences Nouns Nouns: People and Places | | | |
| **TOTAL SCORE** | 29/41 | _____ | _____ |

Were accommodations made in administering this test?  ☐ Yes  ☐ No

Type of accommodations: _____

_____

ISBN 0-15-332156-3

8 9 10   170   10 09 08 07 06 05 04

**DECODING:** Vowels: Phonemes

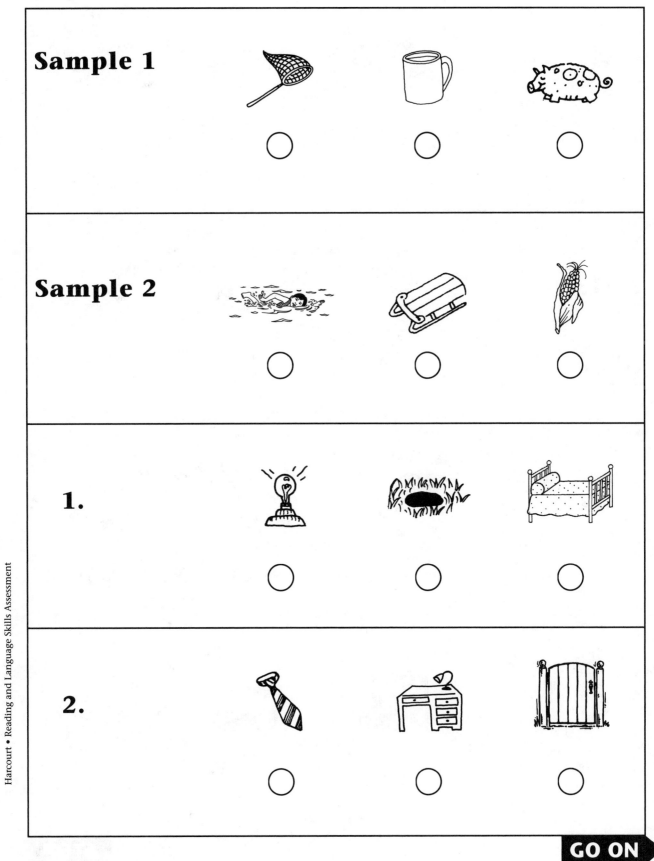

**Sample 1**

○      ○      ○

**Sample 2**

○      ○      ○

**1.**

○      ○      ○

**2.**

○      ○      ○

**GO ON** ▶

**DECODING:** Vowels: Phonemes (continued)

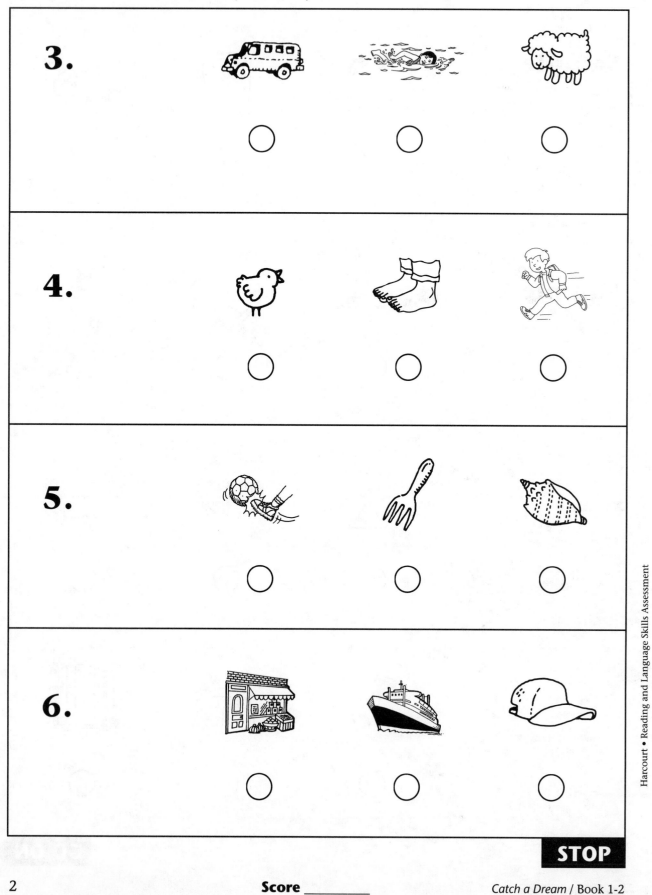

**3.**

**4.**

**5.**

**6.**

**STOP**

**Score** _____

Harcourt • Reading and Language Skills Assessment

**DECODING:** Vowels: Decodable Words

## Sample 1

pet ○   pat ○   pit ○

## Sample 2

stick ○   stork ○   stack ○

**7.** mass ○   mess ○   miss ○

**8.** 10 tan ○   ton ○   ten ○

GO ON ➤

**DECODING:** Vowels: Decodable Words (continued)

**9.** not     net     nut
◯     ◯     ◯

**10.** stick     stuck     stack
◯     ◯     ◯

**11.** horn     hot     hip
◯     ◯     ◯

**12.** snip     snore     snap
◯     ◯     ◯

**STOP**

**Score** _____

*Catch a Dream* / Book 1-2

Harcourt • Reading and Language Skills Assessment

**DECODING:** Initial Blends: Sound-Letter Relationships

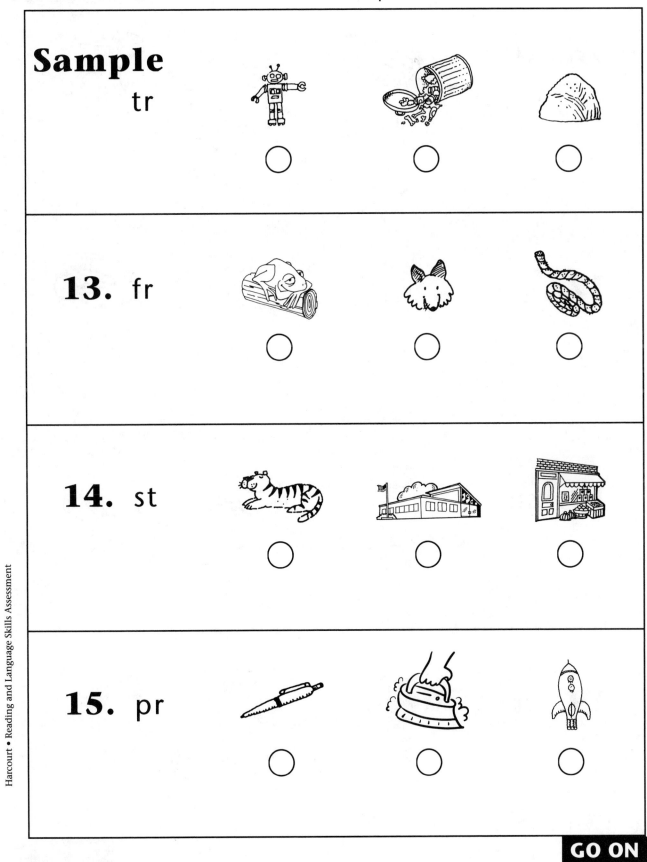

**Sample**
tr

◯   ◯   ◯

**13.** fr

◯   ◯   ◯

**14.** st

◯   ◯   ◯

**15.** pr

◯   ◯   ◯

Harcourt • Reading and Language Skills Assessment

**GO ON**

**DECODING:** Initial Blends: Sound-Letter Relationships (continued)

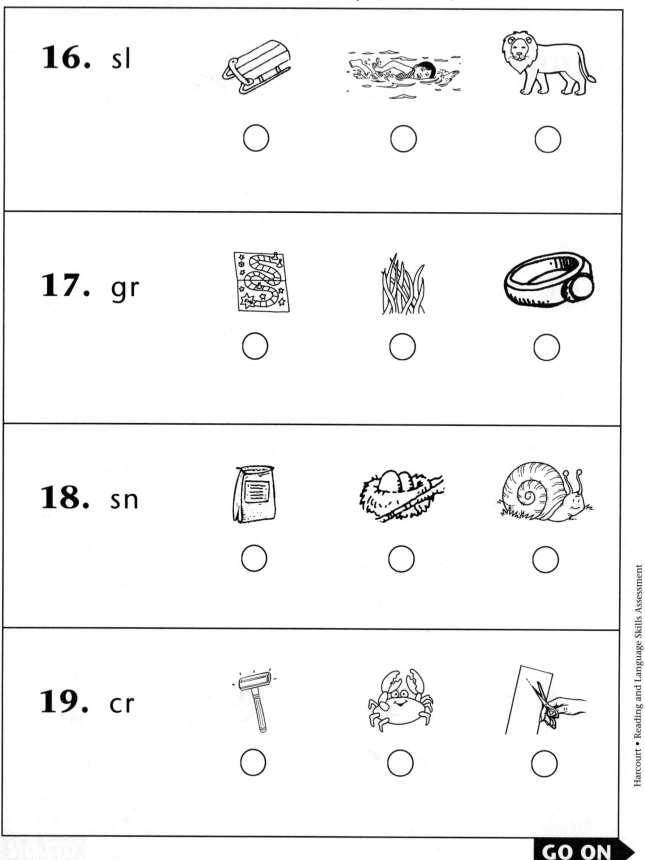

**16.** sl

**17.** gr

**18.** sn

**19.** cr

**GO ON**

Harcourt • Reading and Language Skills Assessment

**DECODING:** Initial Blends: Sound-Letter Relationships (continued)

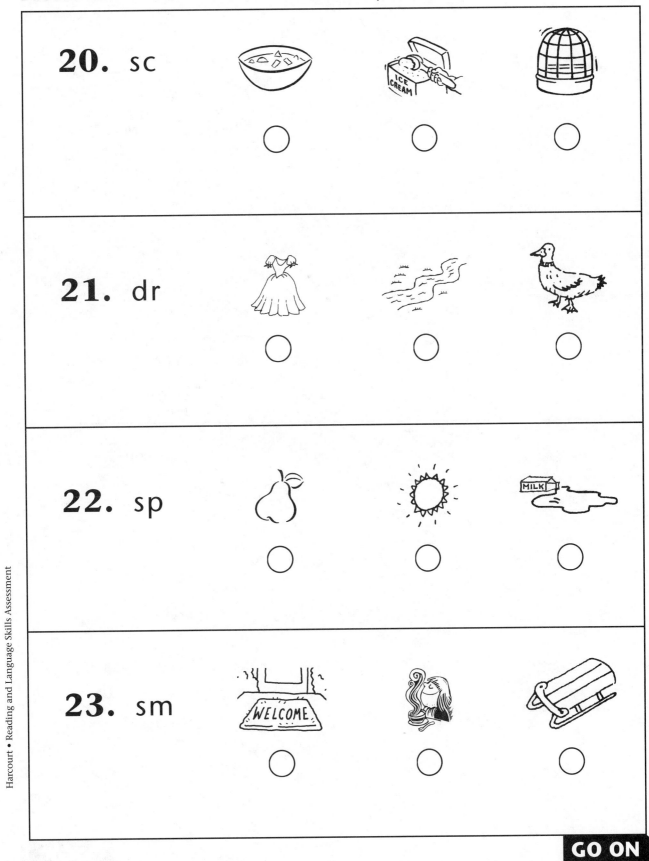

**20.** sc

○   ○   ○

**21.** dr

○   ○   ○

**22.** sp

○   ○   ○

**23.** sm

○   ○   ○

**GO ON**

**DECODING:** Initial Blends: Sound-Letter Relationships (continued)

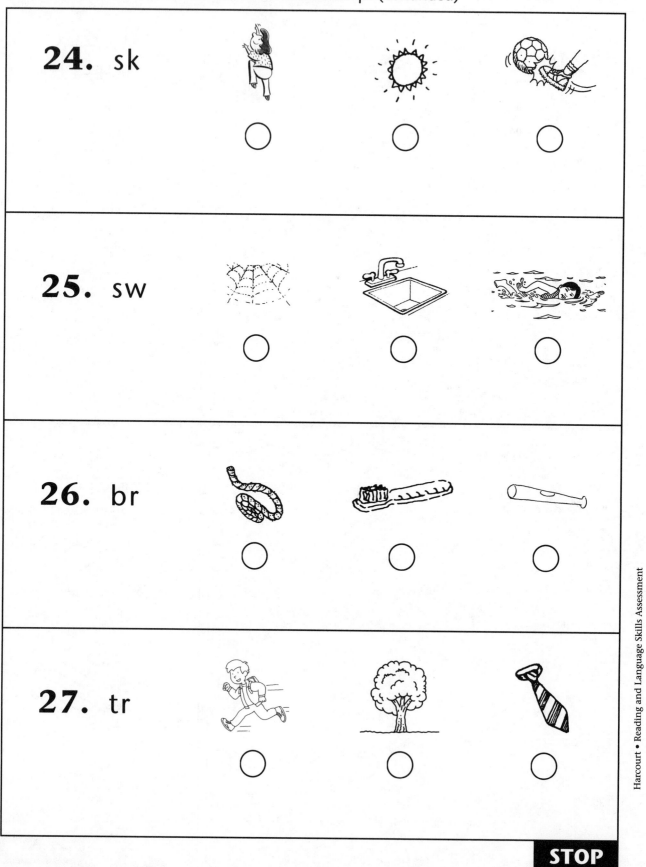

**24.** sk

○　　　　○　　　　○

**25.** sw

○　　　　○　　　　○

**26.** br

○　　　　○　　　　○

**27.** tr

○　　　　○　　　　○

**STOP**

　　　　**Score** _____　　　　*Catch a Dream / Book 1-2*

Harcourt • Reading and Language Skills Assessment

**DECODING:** Digraphs: Sound-Letter Relationships

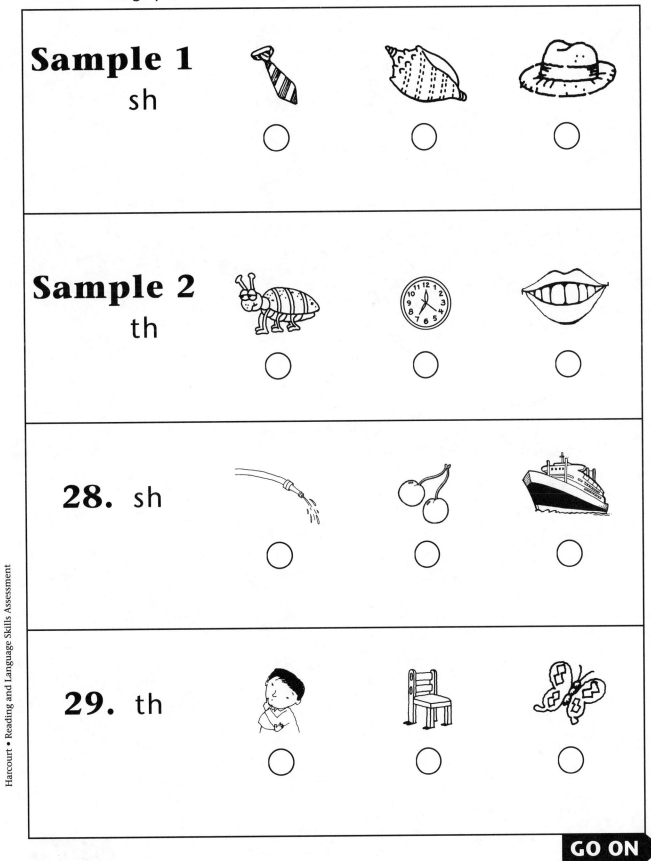

**Sample 1**
sh

○       ○       ○

**Sample 2**
th

○       ○       ○

**28.** sh

○       ○       ○

**29.** th

○       ○       ○

**GO ON**

**DECODING:** Digraphs: Sound-Letter Relationships (continued)

**30.** th

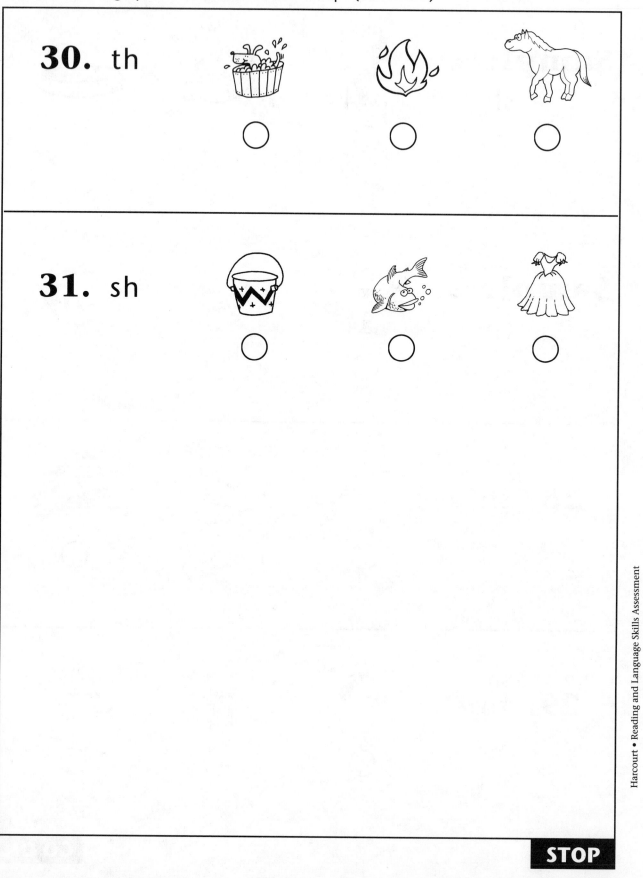

**31.** sh

**STOP**

**Score** _____

*Catch a Dream* / Book 1-2

**COMPREHENSION:** Details

# Sample

## Kim's Cat

Kim has a cat.

She loves her cat.

Each day, Kim pets the cat and plays with the cat.

Every night, she reads to her cat.

What does Kim do with her cat at night?

○ pets her cat

○ reads to her cat

○ plays with her cat

**GO ON**

**COMPREHENSION:** Details (continued)

# Fran's Day at School

Fran walks to school with Dad.
She has on a new dress.
She sees a good friend.
She sees other children.
She sees desks to sit in and games to play.

**32.** Who walks to school with Fran?
- ○ other children
- ○ Dad
- ○ a friend

**33.** What does Fran have that is new?
- ○ a dress
- ○ games
- ○ desks

**GO ON**

Harcourt • Reading and Language Skills Assessment

*Catch a Dream / Book 1-2*

**COMPREHENSION:** Details (continued)

# A Birthday Gift

Dad asked Pat what she wanted for a birthday gift.

She said, "I want a big red bike. I will ride it to school."

Dad said, "I will get you the bike that you want."

**34.** What does Pat want?
- ○ a game
- ○ a hat
- ○ a bike

**35.** What will Pat do with her gift?
- ○ ride it to school
- ○ give it to a friend
- ○ throw it away

**STOP**

**LANGUAGE**

# Sample 1

Sam hits the ball.

naming part      telling part

○            ○

**36.** Pam calls the cat.

naming part      telling part

○            ○

**37.** The dog and cat do tricks.

naming part      telling part

○            ○

**GO ON**

Harcourt • Reading and Language Skills Assessment

**LANGUAGE** (continued)

**38.** Ben <u>slipped and fell.</u>

naming part  telling part

     ○              ○

**GO ON**

**LANGUAGE** (continued)

# Sample 2

He will pick up the rock.

○ will

○ pick

○ rock

**39.** The boy spins a top.

○ boy

○ spins

○ a

**40.** The fish are in a pond.

○ are

○ in

○ pond

**GO ON** ▶

16

Harcourt • Reading and Language Skills Assessment

**LANGUAGE** (continued)

**41.** The doll has a red coat.
- ○ The
- ○ doll
- ○ red

**STOP**

Harcourt • Reading and Language Skills Assessment

· T R O P H I E S ·

# Catch a Dream/Book 1-2
## Reading and Language Skills Assessment

Orlando   Boston   Dallas   Chicago   San Diego

Part No. 9997-37695-1

ISBN 0-15-332156-3  (Package of 12)

1-2

# TROPHIES

# Reading and Language Skills Assessment Posttest

## Catch a Dream/Book 1-2

Name _____ Date _____

| SKILL AREA | Criterion Score | Pupil Score | Pupil Strength |
|---|---|---|---|
| **DECODING** | | | |
| Short Vowels /e/e; /u/u | | | |
| R-controlled Vowels /ôr/or, ore | | | |
| Phonemes | 4/6 | _____ | _____ |
| Decodable Words | 4/6 | _____ | _____ |
| Initial Blends with r and s br, cr, dr, fr, gr, pr, tr sc, sk, sl, sm, sn, sp, st, sw | | | |
| Sound-Letter Relationships | 11/15 | _____ | _____ |
| Digraphs /th/th; /sh/sh | | | |
| Sound-Letter Relationships | 3/4 | _____ | _____ |
| **COMPREHENSION** | | | |
| Details | 3/4 | _____ | _____ |
| **LANGUAGE** | 4/6 | _____ | _____ |
| Naming Parts for Two | | | |
| Telling Parts of Sentences | | | |
| Telling Parts for Two | | | |
| Complete Sentences | | | |
| Nouns | | | |
| Nouns: People and Places | | | |
| **TOTAL SCORE** | 29/41 | _____ | _____ |

Were accommodations made in administering this test?  ❑ Yes   ❑ No

Type of accommodations: _____

_____

Printed in the United States of America

ISBN 0-15-332156-3

8 9 10   170   10 09 08 07 06 05 04

**DECODING:** Vowels: Phonemes

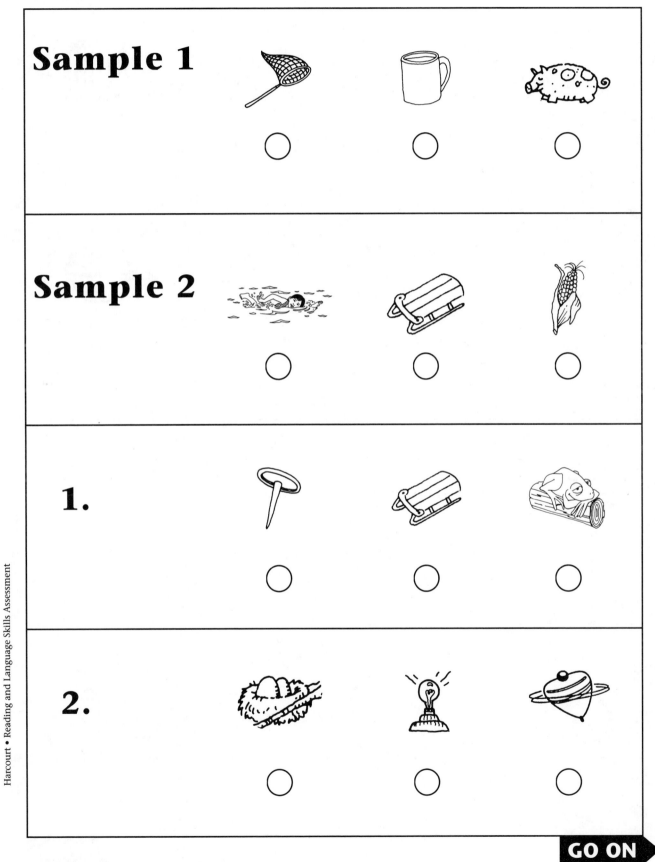

**Sample 1**

○    ○    ○

**Sample 2**

○    ○    ○

**1.**

○    ○    ○

**2.**

○    ○    ○

**GO ON**

Harcourt • Reading and Language Skills Assessment

**DECODING:** Vowels: Phonemes (continued)

3.

○       ○       ○

4.

○       ○       ○

5.

○       ○       ○

6.

○       ○       ○

**STOP**

**Score** _____       *Catch a Dream* / Book 1-2

**DECODING:** Vowels: Decodable Words

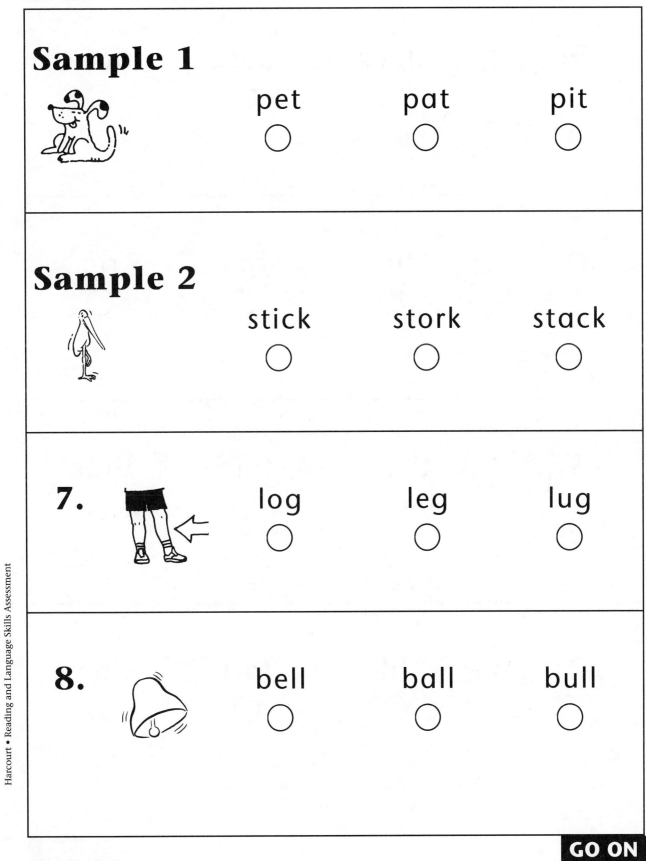

## Sample 1

pet          pat          pit
○            ○            ○

## Sample 2

stick        stork        stack
○            ○            ○

**7.**       log          leg          lug
○            ○            ○

**8.**       bell         ball         bull
○            ○            ○

**GO ON**

**DECODING:** Vowels: Decodable Words (continued)

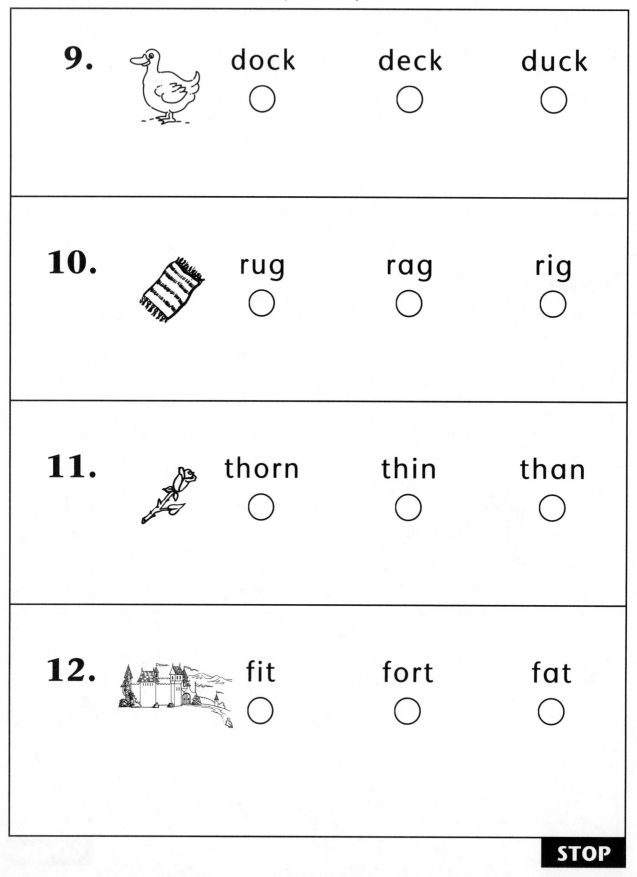

**9.**    dock     deck     duck
      ◯      ◯      ◯

**10.**    rug     rag     rig
      ◯      ◯      ◯

**11.**    thorn     thin     than
      ◯      ◯      ◯

**12.**    fit     fort     fat
      ◯      ◯      ◯

**STOP**

Harcourt • Reading and Language Skills Assessment

**DECODING:** Initial Blends: Sound-Letter Relationships

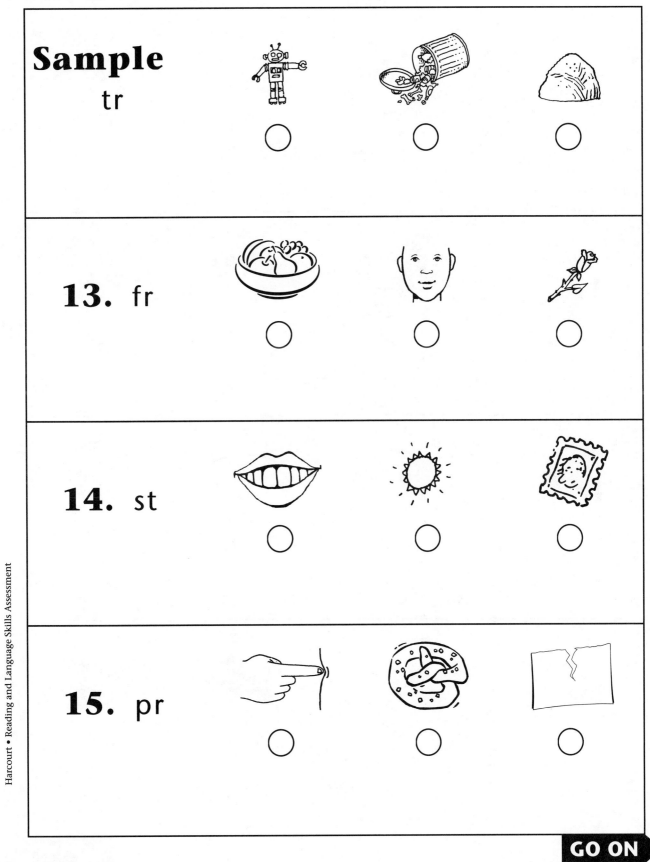

**Sample**

tr

○          ○          ○

**13.** fr

○          ○          ○

**14.** st

○          ○          ○

**15.** pr

○          ○          ○

**GO ON**

**DECODING:** Initial Blends: Sound-Letter Relationships (continued)

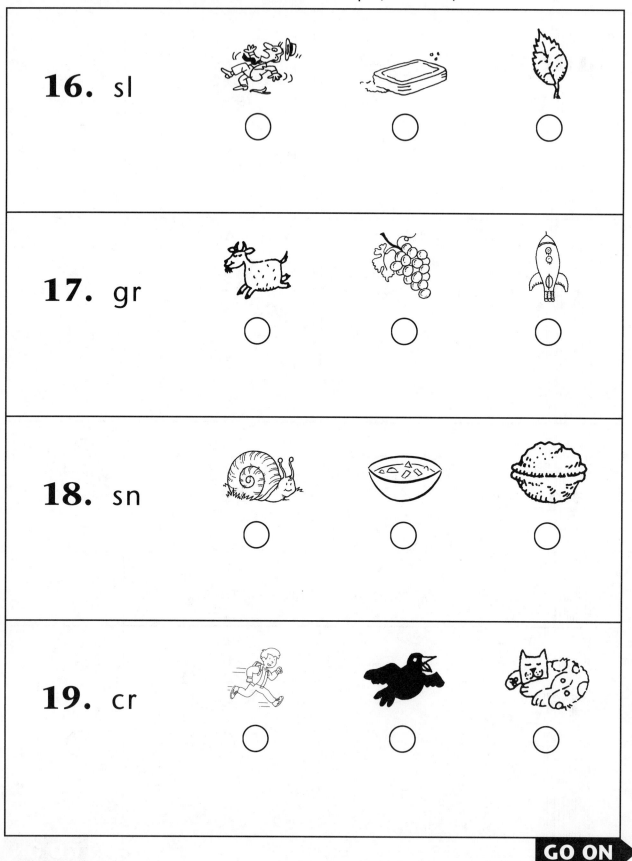

**16.** sl

**17.** gr

**18.** sn

**19.** cr

**GO ON**

**DECODING:** Initial Blends: Sound-Letter Relationships (continued)

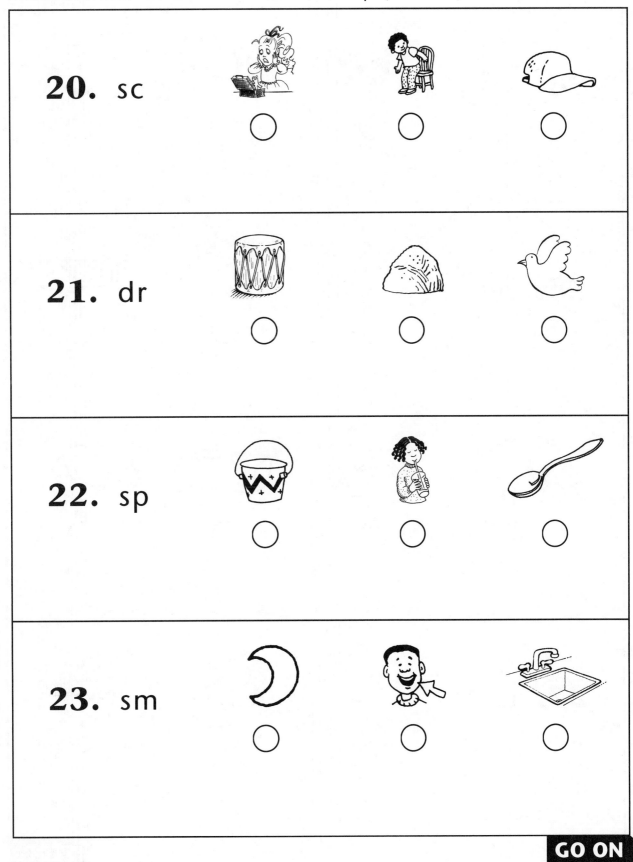

**20.** sc     ◯        ◯        ◯

**21.** dr     ◯        ◯        ◯

**22.** sp     ◯        ◯        ◯

**23.** sm     ◯        ◯        ◯

**GO ON**

**DECODING:** Initial Blends: Sound-Letter Relationships (continued)

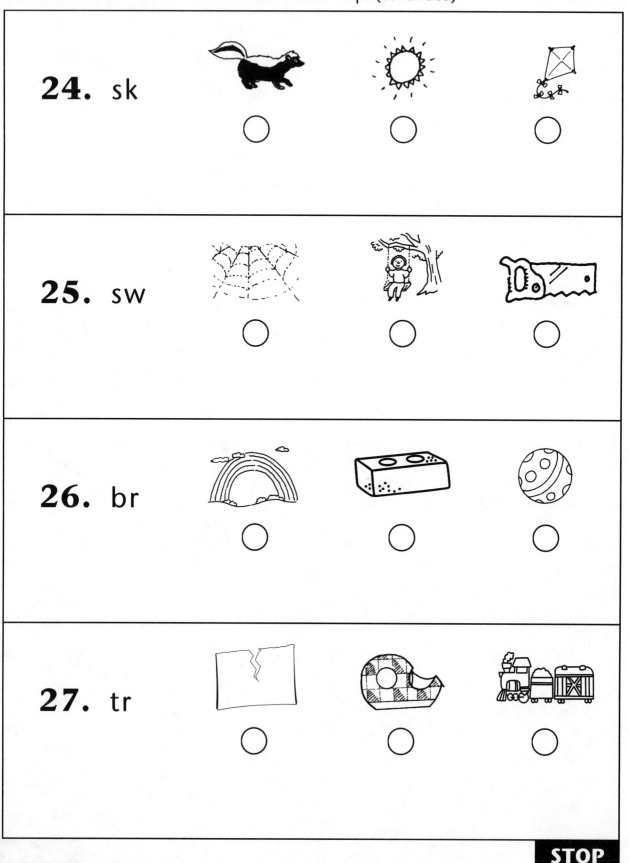

**24.** sk

   ○      ○      ○

**25.** sw

   ○      ○      ○

**26.** br

   ○      ○      ○

**27.** tr

   ○      ○      ○

**STOP**

Harcourt • Reading and Language Skills Assessment

**DECODING:** Digraphs: Sound-Letter Relationships

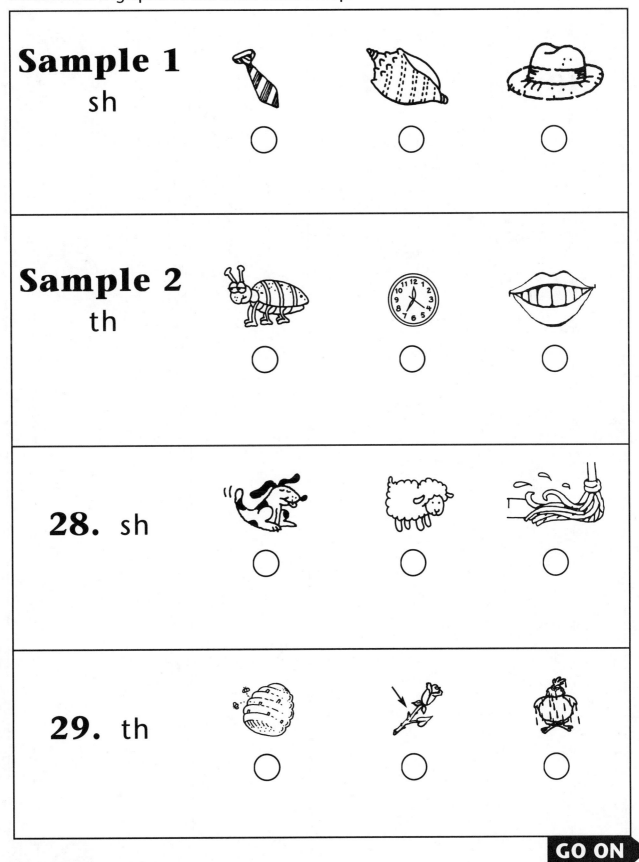

**Sample 1**
sh

○    ○    ○

**Sample 2**
th

○    ○    ○

**28.** sh

○    ○    ○

**29.** th

○    ○    ○

**GO ON**

**DECODING:** Digraphs: Sound-Letter Relationships (continued)

**30.** th

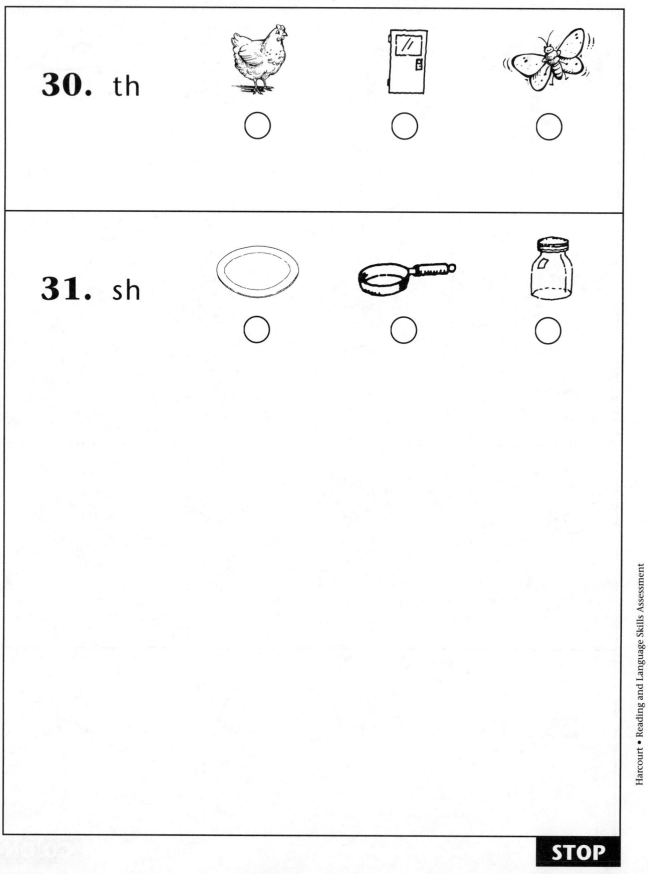

○  ○  ○

**31.** sh

○  ○  ○

**STOP**

**Score** _____

*Catch a Dream* / Book 1-2

**COMPREHENSION:** Details

# Sample

## Kim's Cat

Kim has a cat.
She loves her cat.
Each day, Kim pets the cat and
plays with the cat.
Every night, she reads to her cat.

What does Kim do with her cat at
night?

○  pets her cat

○  reads to her cat

○  plays with her cat

**GO ON**

# A Hot Day

It was a very hot day.
Carl and his friends wanted to play in the water.
Carl's Mom came outside.
She gave the children cold juice to drink.
She said she would take them to the city pool.
Carl ran to tell Dad where they were going.

**GO ON**

Harcourt • Reading and Language Skills Assessment

**COMPREHENSION:** Details (continued)

**32.** Who wants to play in the water?
  ○ Mom
  ○ Carl
  ○ Dad

**33.** What do the children get to drink?
  ○ milk
  ○ water
  ○ juice

**STOP**

Harcourt • Reading and Language Skills Assessment

# Picking Flowers

Sara goes out to pick flowers in her yard.

She sees roses, lilies, pansies, and buttercups.

Sara picks four red roses to give to Grandma.

Roses are Grandma's favorite flower.

**34.** Which flower does Sara pick?
○ lilies
○ pansies
○ roses

**COMPREHENSION:** Details (continued)

**35.** How many flowers will Sara give Grandma?

○ one

○ three

○ four

**STOP**

**LANGUAGE** (continued)

# Sample 1

Sam hits the ball.

○ naming part      ○ telling part

**36.** That pot is hot.

○ naming part      ○ telling part

**37.** My friend and I play ball.

○ naming part      ○ telling part

**38.** Jan ran and jumped.

○ naming part      ○ telling part

**GO ON**

*Catch a Dream / Book 1-2*

Harcourt • Reading and Language Skills Assessment

**LANGUAGE** (continued)

## Sample 2

He will pick up the rock.

○ will

○ pick

○ rock

**39.** The girl has a penny.

○ girl

○ has

○ a

**40.** The pigs are in a pen.

○ are

○ in

○ pen

**GO ON**

**LANGUAGE** (continued)

**41.** The truck has a loud horn.
- ○ The
- ○ truck
- ○ loud

**STOP**

**Score** _____

*Catch a Dream* / Book 1-2

· T R O P H I E S ·

# Catch a Dream/Book 1-2

## Reading and Language Skills Assessment

**Harcourt**

Orlando   Boston   Dallas   Chicago   San Diego

Part No. 9997-37696-X

ISBN 0-15-332156-3  (Package of 12)

1-2

# TROPHIES

# Reading and Language Skills Assessment Pretest

## Here and There/Book 1-3

Name _____ Date _____

| SKILL AREA | Criterion Score | Pupil Score | Pupil Strength |
|---|---|---|---|
| **DECODING** | | | |
| Long Vowels | | | |
| /ō/ow, oa | | | |
| R-controlled Vowels | | | |
| /är/ar | | | |
| /ûr/er, ir, ur | | | |
| Phonemes | 4/6 | _____ | _____ |
| Decodable Words | 4/6 | _____ | _____ |
| Blends | | | |
| Initial Blends with l | | | |
| bl, cl, fl, gl, pl, sl | | | |
| Sound-Letter Relationships | 4/6 | _____ | _____ |
| Digraphs | | | |
| /ch/ch, tch; /kw/qu; /hw/wh | | | |
| Sound-Letter Relationships | 4/6 | _____ | _____ |
| Inflections | | | |
| -s, -ed, -ing | | | |
| (no spelling change) | 3/4 | _____ | _____ |
| | | | |
| **COMPREHENSION** | | | |
| Setting and Character | 4/6 | _____ | _____ |
| | | | |
| **LANGUAGE** | 4/6 | _____ | _____ |
| Nouns: Animals and Things | | | |
| Special Names and Titles for People | | | |
| Special Names for Places | | | |
| | | | |
| **TOTAL SCORE** | 27/40 | _____ | _____ |

Were accommodations made in administering this test?  ☐ Yes  ☐ No

Type of accommodations: _____

_____

Printed in the United States of America

ISBN 0-15-332164-4

8 9 10 170 10 09 08 07 06 05 04

**DECODING:** Vowels: Phonemes

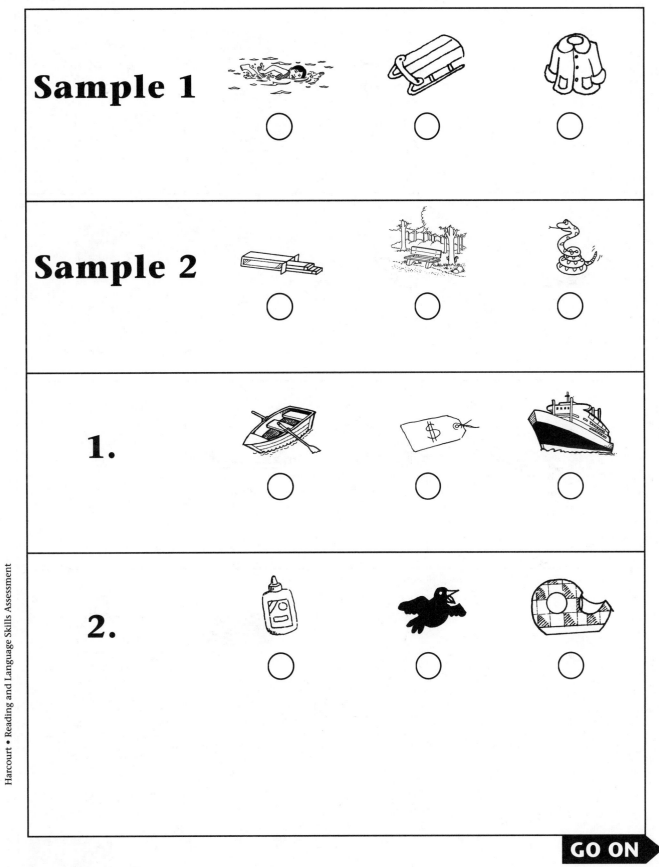

Sample 1

○　　　　○　　　　○

Sample 2

○　　　　○　　　　○

1.

○　　　　○　　　　○

2.

○　　　　○　　　　○

**GO ON** ▶

**DECODING:** Vowels: Phonemes (continued)

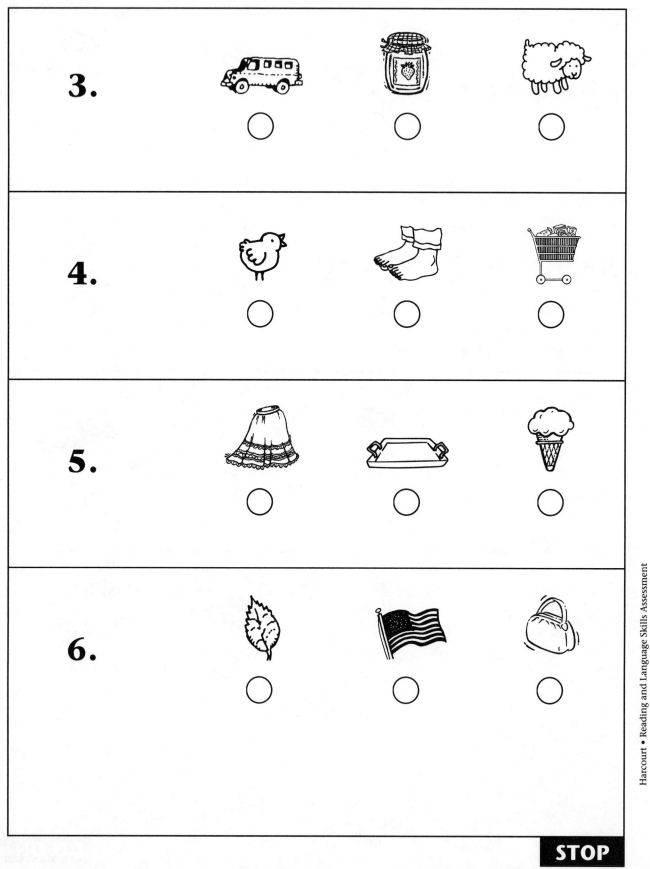

**3.**

○      ○      ○

**4.**

○      ○      ○

**5.**

○      ○      ○

**6.**

○      ○      ○

**STOP**

**Score** _____

Harcourt • Reading and Language Skills Assessment

**DECODING:** Vowels: Decodable Words

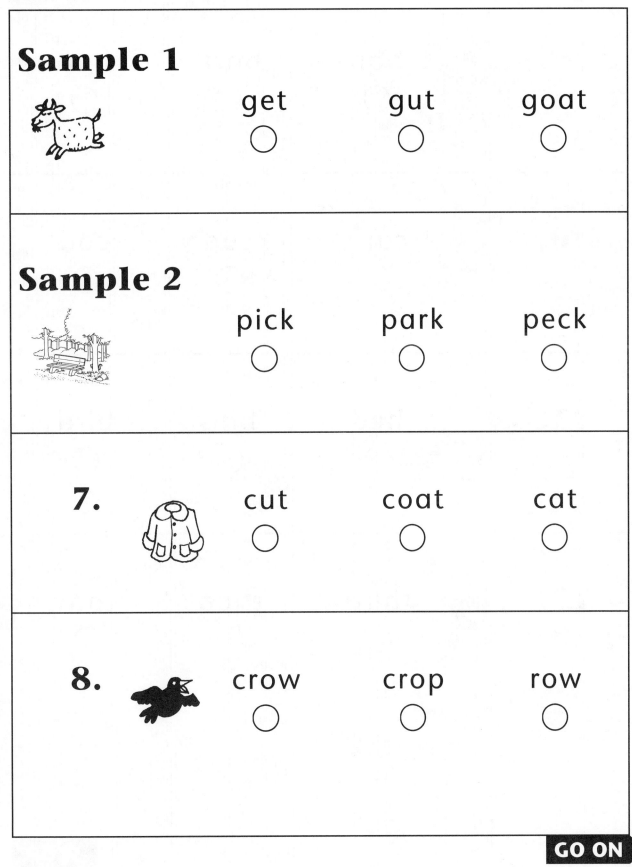

# Sample 1

get ◯     gut ◯     goat ◯

# Sample 2

pick ◯     park ◯     peck ◯

**7.**

cut ◯     coat ◯     cat ◯

**8.**

crow ◯     crop ◯     row ◯

**GO ON**

Harcourt • Reading and Language Skills Assessment

**DECODING:** Vowels: Decodable Words (continued)

**9.**     ban     barn     bun
    ○     ○     ○

**10.**     card     cud     cod
    ○     ○     ○

**11.**     bed     bad     bird
    ○     ○     ○

**12.**  **3**  third     thud     that
    ○     ○     ○

**STOP**

Harcourt • Reading and Language Skills Assessment

**DECODING:** Initial Blends: Sound-Letter Relationships

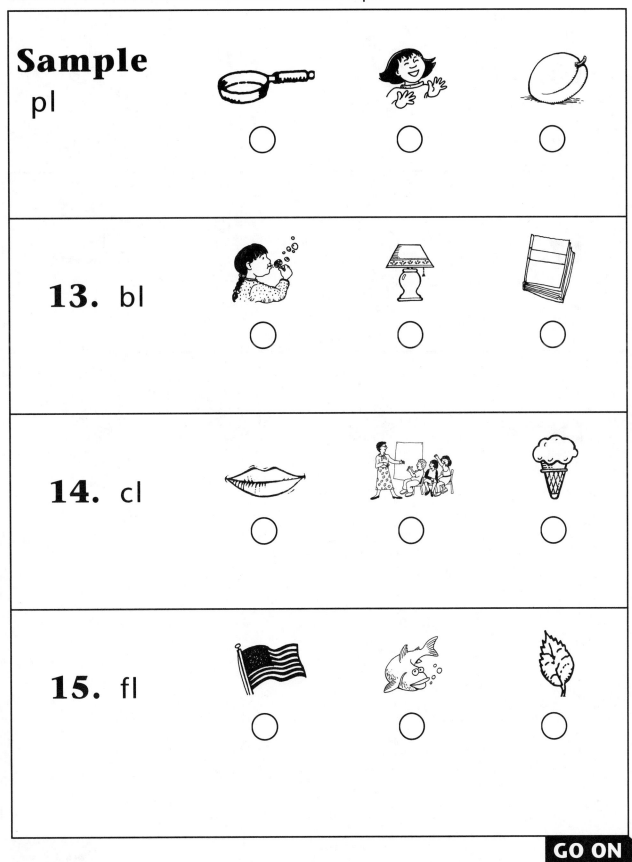

**Sample**

pl

**13.** bl

**14.** cl

**15.** fl

**GO ON**

**DECODING:** Initial Blends: Sound-Letter Relationships (continued)

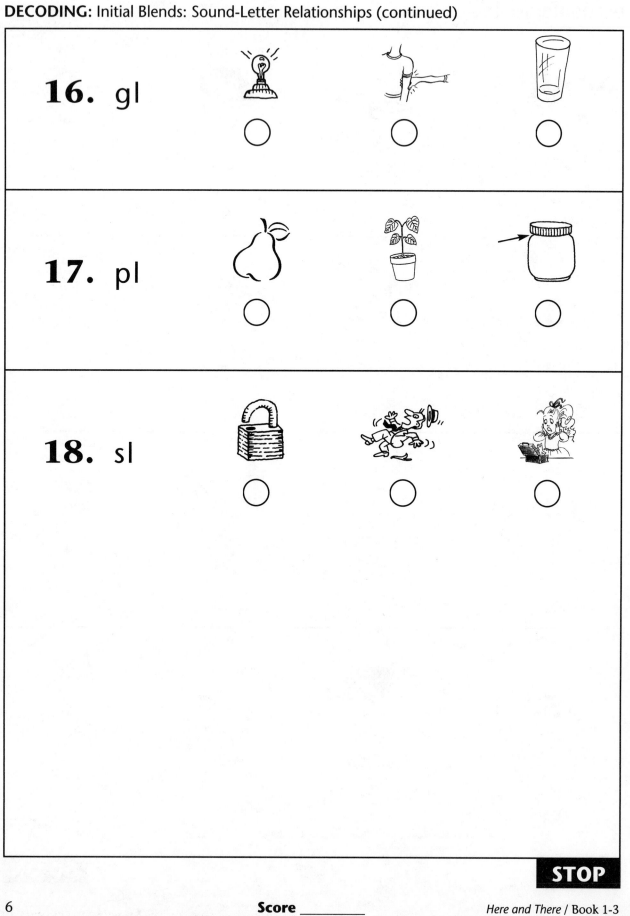

**16.** gl

○    ○    ○

**17.** pl

○    ○    ○

**18.** sl

○    ○    ○

**STOP**

**Score** _____    *Here and There / Book 1-3*

Harcourt • Reading and Language Skills Assessment

**DECODING:** Digraphs: Sound-Letter Relationships

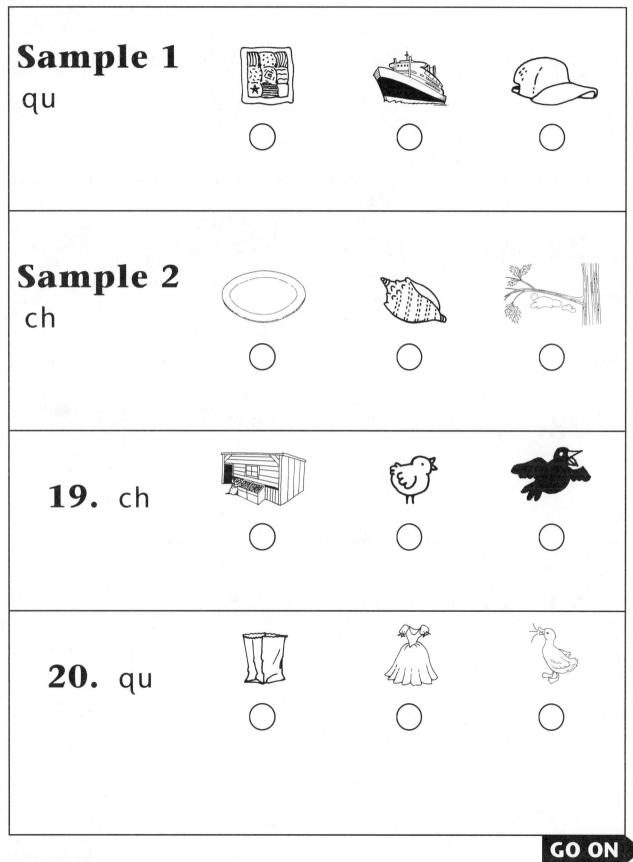

**Sample 1**
qu

○   ○   ○

**Sample 2**
ch

○   ○   ○

**19.** ch

○   ○   ○

**20.** qu

○   ○   ○

**GO ON**

Harcourt • Reading and Language Skills Assessment

**DECODING:** Digraphs: Sound-Letter Relationships  (continued)

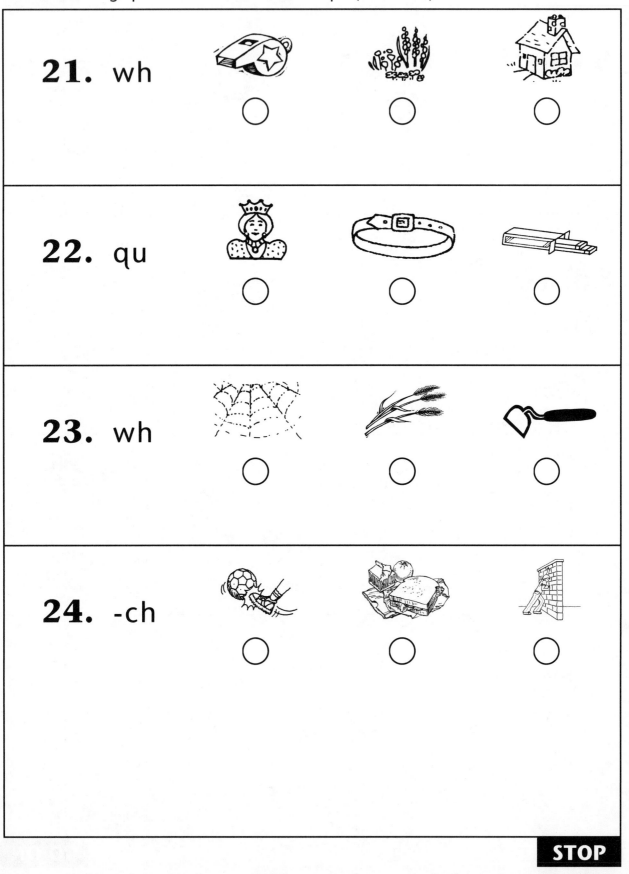

**21.** wh    ⚪    ⚪    ⚪

**22.** qu    ⚪    ⚪    ⚪

**23.** wh    ⚪    ⚪    ⚪

**24.** -ch    ⚪    ⚪    ⚪

**STOP**

Harcourt • Reading and Language Skills Assessment

**DECODING:** Inflections

## Sample

He _____ the ball.

|  kick  |  kicked  |  kicking  |
|:---:|:---:|:---:|
| ○ | ○ | ○ |

**25.** The boat is _____.

|  sink  |  sinks  |  sinking  |
|:---:|:---:|:---:|
| ○ | ○ | ○ |

**26.** We _____ for the lost book.

|  looked  |  looks  |  looking  |
|:---:|:---:|:---:|
| ○ | ○ | ○ |

**27.** Dad is _____ Sam.

|  call  |  calls  |  calling  |
|:---:|:---:|:---:|
| ○ | ○ | ○ |

**28.** Fran _____ her lunch.

|  pack  |  packs  |  packing  |
|:---:|:---:|:---:|
| ○ | ○ | ○ |

**STOP**

**COMPREHENSION:** Setting and Character

# Sample

## Ben Plays Ball

One day, Ben went to Sam's house. Sam got a bat, and Ben got a ball. They played ball and had fun.

Where does this story take place?

○ in a barn

○ at a store

○ at Sam's house

**COMPREHENSION:** Setting and Character (continued)

# Farm Trip

It was a warm spring day.

Mom and Ann went to Mr. Hall's farm.

Ann saw pigs and horses at the farm.

She saw little chicks and a big hen.

Ann said, "I want to come back soon."

**29.** Where did this story take place?

○ at school

○ on a farm

○ in a house

**GO ON**

**COMPREHENSION:** Setting and Character (continued)

**30.** When did this story take place?

○ spring

○ winter

○ fall

**31.** Who is this story about?

○ Mom

○ Ann, Mom, and Mr. Hall

○ Mr. Hall

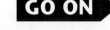

GO ON

*Here and There / Book 1-3*

**COMPREHENSION:** Setting and Character (continued)

# Fun at the Pond

One hot summer day, Fran Frog bumped into Tom Toad.

She said, "Won't you come to my pond?"

Tom said, "Yes."

Fran and Tom had a big lunch.

Alvin Ant had lunch with them.

Then Fran and Tom splashed in the pond.

Last, they jumped up on a rock and sat in the sun.

**32.** Where did this story take place?

○ at Tom's house

○ at Fran's pond

○ at a pet shop

**GO ON**

Harcourt • Reading and Language Skills Assessment

**COMPREHENSION:** Setting and Character (continued)

**33.** When did this story take place?

  ○  at lunch time

  ○  at bed time

  ○  at night

**34.** Who had lunch with Fran and Tom?

  ○  a fish

  ○  a duck

  ○  an ant

**STOP**

Harcourt • Reading and Language Skills Assessment

# Sample 1

She will throw the ball.

○ will

○ throw

○ ball

**35.** The pig is in a pen.

○ pig

○ is

○ in

**36.** I see a pretty horse.

○ see

○ a

○ horse

**GO ON**

# Sample 2

My teacher is Mr. Simms.

- ○ my
- ○ is
- ○ Mr. Simms

**37.** Mr. Smith is my friend.

- ○ Mr. Smith
- ○ is
- ○ my

**38.** We live on Hill Street.

- ○ live
- ○ on
- ○ Hill Street

**GO ON**

**LANGUAGE** (continued)

**39.** Soon Uncle Ned will be here.
- ○ Soon
- ○ Uncle Ned
- ○ be

**40.** We are going to Sun Park.
- ○ are
- ○ to
- ○ Sun Park

**STOP**

# TROPHIES

## Here and There / Book 1-3
## Reading and Language Skills Assessment

Orlando   Boston   Dallas   Chicago   San Diego

Part No. 9997-37698-6

ISBN 0-15-332164-4  (Package of 12)

1-3

# · T R O P H I E S ·

# Reading and Language Skills Assessment Posttest

## Here and There/Book 1-3

Name _____ Date _____

| SKILL AREA | Criterion Score | Pupil Score | Pupil Strength |
|---|---|---|---|
| **DECODING** | | | |
| Long Vowels | | | |
| /ō/ow, oa | | | |
| R-controlled Vowels | | | |
| /är/ar | | | |
| /ûr/er, ir, ur | | | |
| Phonemes | 4/6 | _____ | _____ |
| Decodable Words | 4/6 | _____ | _____ |
| Blends | | | |
| Initial Blends with l | | | |
| bl, cl, fl, gl, pl, sl | | | |
| Sound-Letter Relationships | 4/6 | _____ | _____ |
| Digraphs | | | |
| /ch/ch, tch; /kw/qu; /hw/wh | | | |
| Sound-Letter Relationships | 4/6 | _____ | _____ |
| Inflections | | | |
| -s, -ed, -ing | | | |
| (no spelling change) | 3/4 | _____ | _____ |
| | | | |
| **COMPREHENSION** | | | |
| Setting and Character | 4/6 | _____ | _____ |
| | | | |
| **LANGUAGE** | 4/6 | _____ | _____ |
| Nouns: Animals and Things | | | |
| Special Names and Titles for People | | | |
| Special Names for Places | | | |
| | | | |
| **TOTAL SCORE** | 27/40 | _____ | _____ |

Were accommodations made in administering this test?  ☐ Yes   ☐ No

Type of accommodations: _____

_____

**DECODING:** Vowels: Phonemes

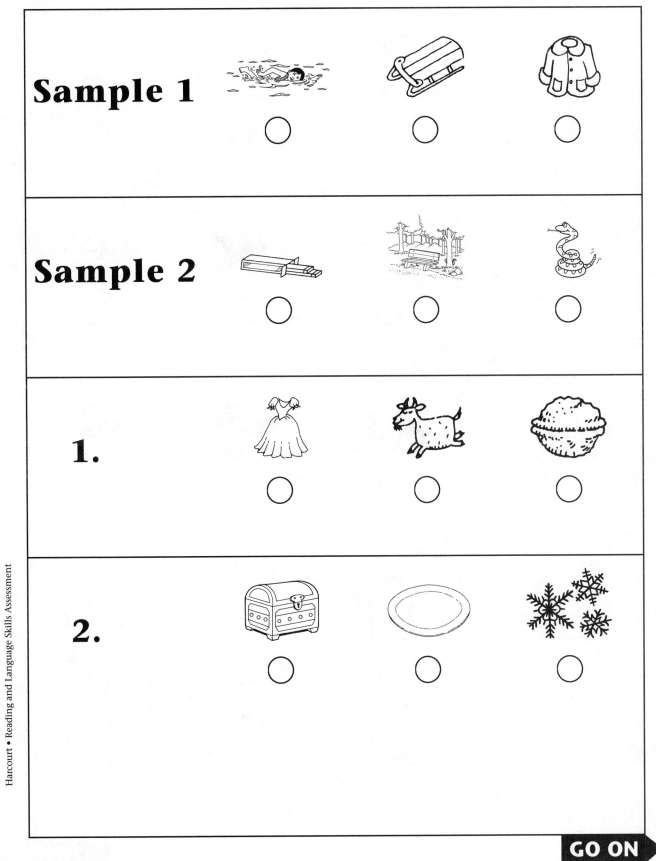

Sample 1

○          ○          ○

Sample 2

○          ○          ○

1.

○          ○          ○

2.

○          ○          ○

**GO ON**

**DECODING:** Vowels: Phonemes

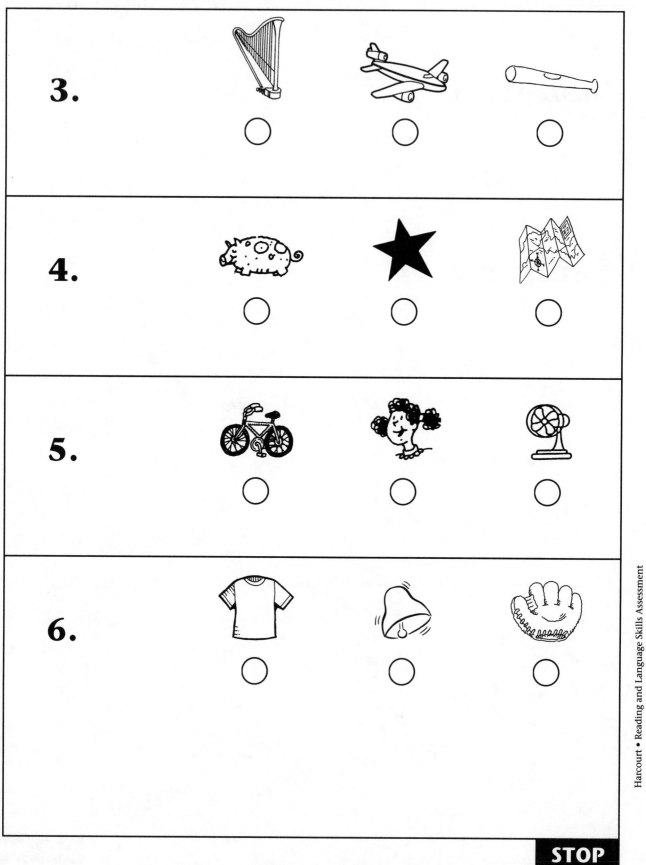

**3.**

**4.**

**5.**

**6.**

**STOP**

**Score** _____

Harcourt • Reading and Language Skills Assessment

**DECODING:** Vowels: Decodable Words

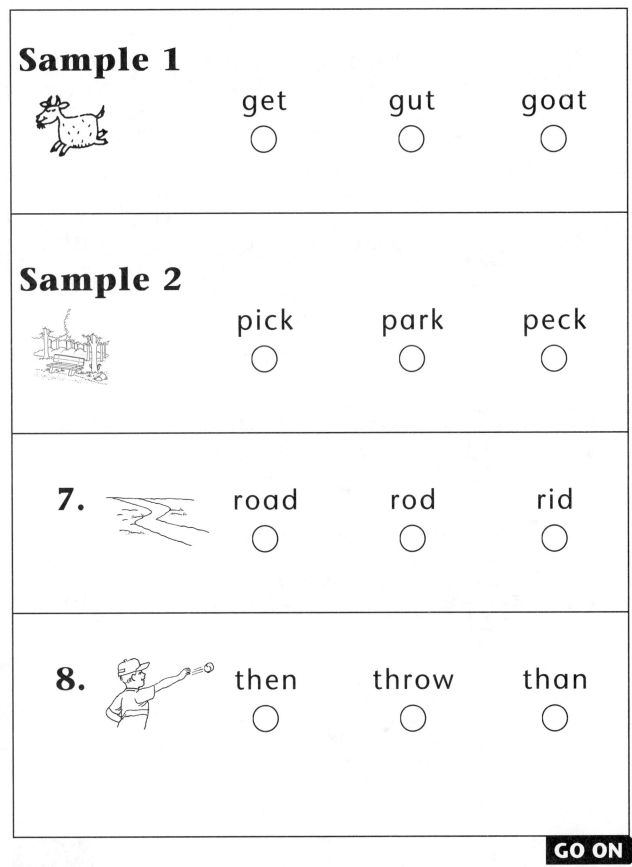

# Sample 1

get       gut       goat

○       ○       ○

# Sample 2

pick       park       peck

○       ○       ○

**7.** road       rod       rid

○       ○       ○

**8.** then       throw       than

○       ○       ○

**GO ON**

**DECODING:** Vowels: Decodable Words (continued)

**9.**   hop ○    hip ○    harp ○

**10.**  cut ○    cart ○    cat ○

**11.**  fist ○    first ○    fast ○

**12.**  girl ○    gull ○    gill ○

**STOP**

Harcourt • Reading and Language Skills Assessment

**DECODING:** Initial Blends: Sound-Letter Relationships

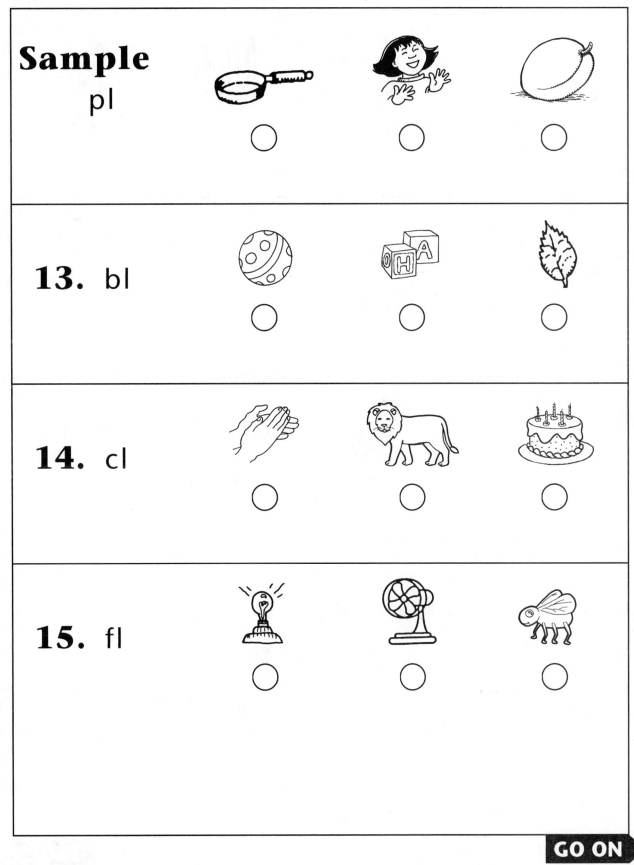

**Sample**
pl

**13.** bl

**14.** cl

**15.** fl

**GO ON**

**DECODING:** Initial Blends: Sound-Letter Relationships (continued)

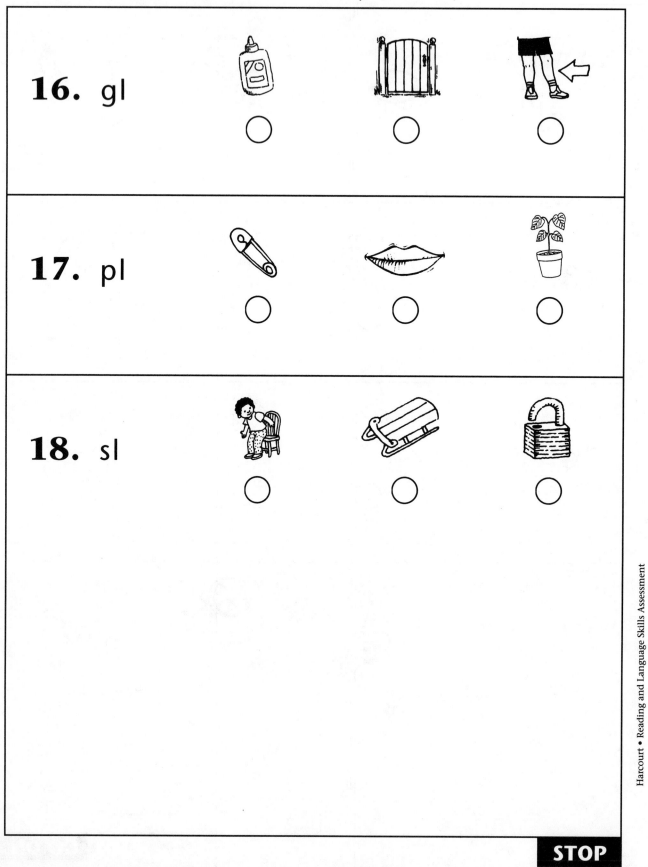

**16.** gl

○          ○          ○

**17.** pl

○          ○          ○

**18.** sl

○          ○          ○

**Score** _____

**STOP**

Harcourt • Reading and Language Skills Assessment

**DECODING:** Digraphs: Sound-Letter Relationships

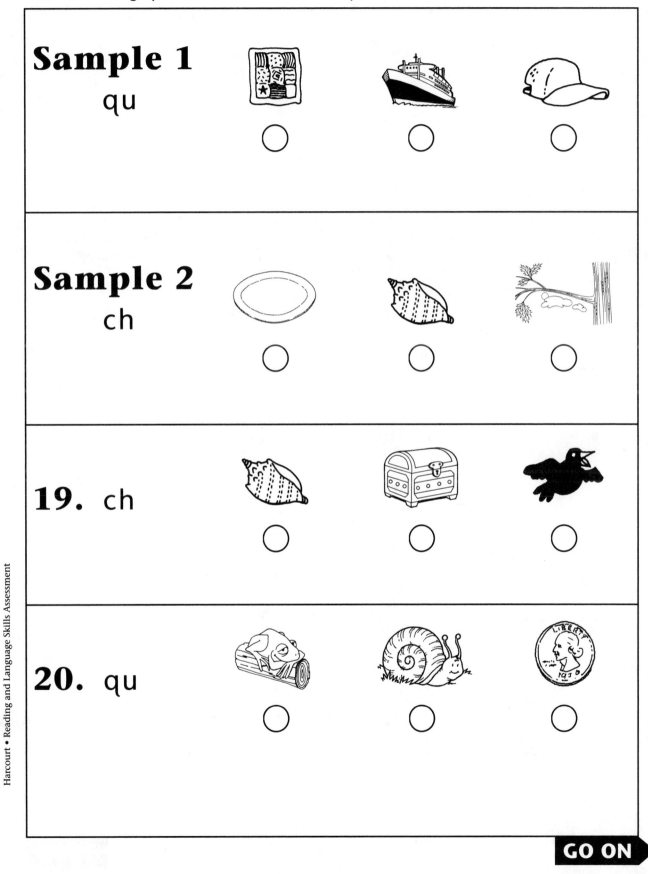

**Sample 1**
qu

○   ○   ○

**Sample 2**
ch

○   ○   ○

**19.** ch

○   ○   ○

**20.** qu

○   ○   ○

**GO ON** ▶

**DECODING:** Digraphs: Sound-Letter Relationships (continued)

**21.** wh

**22.** qu

**23.** wh

**24.** -tch

Harcourt • Reading and Language Skills Assessment

**STOP**

**Score** _____     *Here and There* / Book 1-3

Name _____Skills Assessment

**DECODING:** Inflections

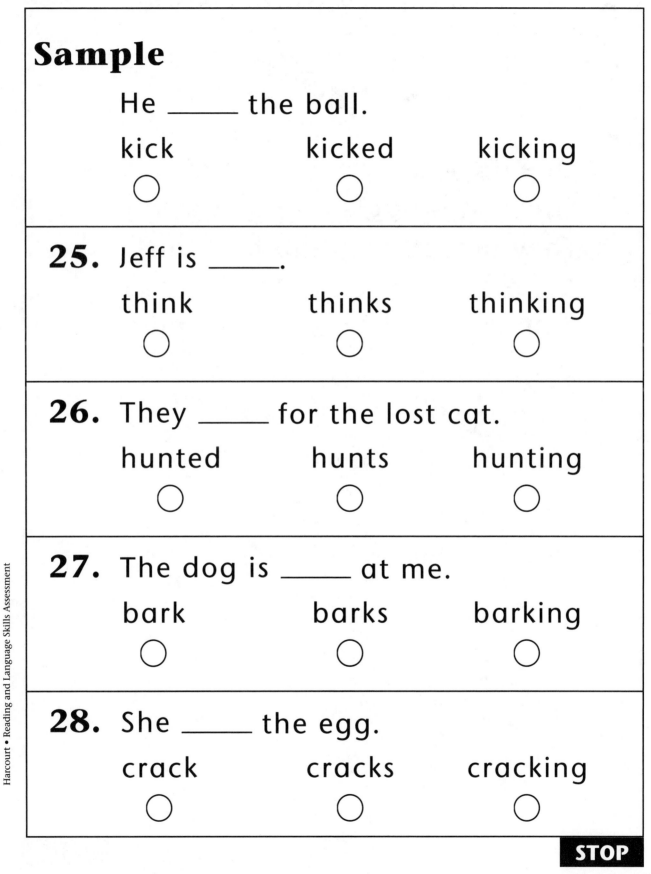

**Sample**

He _____ the ball.

kick                    kicked                  kicking
○                      ○                      ○

**25.** Jeff is _____.

think                  thinks                  thinking
○                      ○                      ○

**26.** They _____ for the lost cat.

hunted                 hunts                   hunting
○                      ○                      ○

**27.** The dog is _____ at me.

bark                   barks                   barking
○                      ○                      ○

**28.** She _____ the egg.

crack                  cracks                  cracking
○                      ○                      ○

**STOP**

Harcourt • Reading and Language Skills Assessment

**COMPREHENSION:** Setting and Character

# Sample

## Ben Plays Ball

One day, Ben went to Sam's house. Sam got a bat, and Ben got a ball. They played ball and had fun.

Where does this story take place?
- ○ in a barn
- ○ at a store
- ○ at Sam's house

*Here and There / Book 1-3*

**COMPREHENSION: Setting and Character (continued)**

# Meg and Champ

Champ, Meg's cat, curled up on the bed next to Meg one night. He let her pet his soft fur. Then he purred and stretched his long tail. Soon Champ quit purring. He slept by Meg all night.

**29.** Where did this story take place?

- ⃝  on a bed
- ⃝  in the grass
- ⃝  on a park bench

**GO ON**

**COMPREHENSION:** Setting and Character (continued)

**30.** When did this story take place?

○ in the morning

○ at lunch

○ at night

**31.** Who is Champ?

○ Meg's mom

○ Meg's cat

○ Meg's sister

# Show and Tell

The bell rings.
Carl and Sal go in.
This morning, Carl will show his pet turtle to the class.
Sal will tell about her trip to a farm.
Carl and Sal are glad they get to show and tell things at school.

**32.** Where did this story take place?
- ○ on a farm
- ○ at school
- ○ at Carl's house

**GO ON**

**COMPREHENSION:** Setting and Character (continued)

**33.** When did this story take place?

○ at night

○ at bed time

○ in the morning

**34.** Who will tell about a trip?

○ Sal

○ Carl

○ the class

**STOP**

**Score** _____

Harcourt • Reading and Language Skills Assessment

**LANGUAGE**

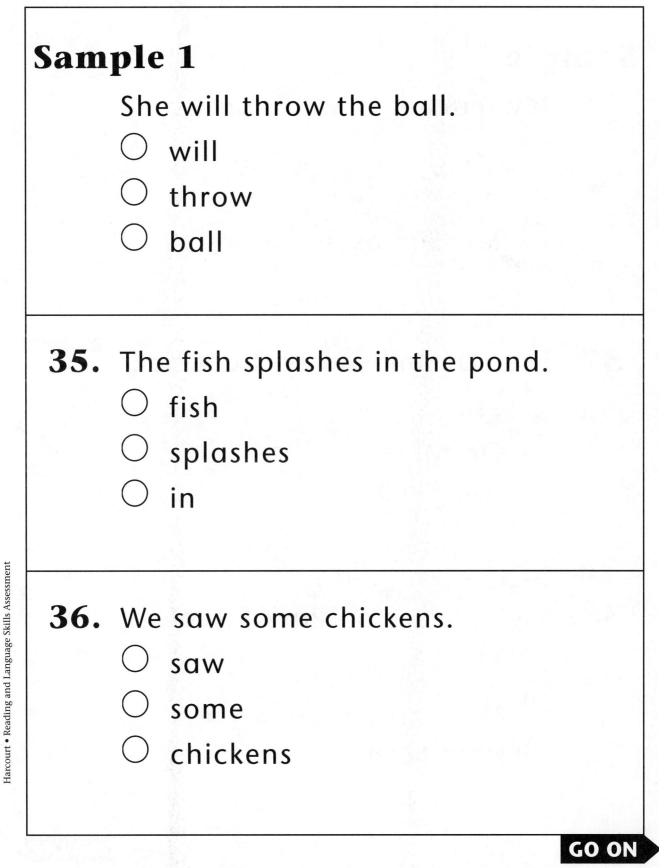

## Sample 1

She will throw the ball.

- ○ will
- ○ throw
- ○ ball

**35.** The fish splashes in the pond.

- ○ fish
- ○ splashes
- ○ in

**36.** We saw some chickens.

- ○ saw
- ○ some
- ○ chickens

**GO ON**

Harcourt • Reading and Language Skills Assessment

# Sample 2

My teacher is Mr. Simms.

○ my

○ is

○ Mr. Simms

**37.** I see Dr. Mills when I am sick.

○ see

○ Dr. Mills

○ am

**38.** My house is on Park Street.

○ My

○ is

○ Park Street

**GO ON**

Harcourt • Reading and Language Skills Assessment

**LANGUAGE** (continued)

**39.** Soon Mrs. Conn will be here.

○ Soon

○ Mrs. Conn

○ be

**40.** We had fun at Pebble Pond.

○ had

○ at

○ Pebble Pond

**STOP**

# • TROPHIES •

## Here and There / Book 1-3
## Reading and Language Skills Assessment

**Harcourt**

Orlando   Boston   Dallas   Chicago   San Diego

Part No. 9997-37699-4

ISBN 0-15-332164-4  (Package of 12)

1-3

# TROPHIES

# Mid-Year Reading and Language Skills Assessment

## Books 1-1, 1-2, 1-3

Name_____ Date_____

| SKILL AREA | Criterion Score | Pupil Score | Comments |
|---|---|---|---|
| DECODING/PHONICS | 26/34 | _____ | _____ |
| COMPREHENSION | 6/8 | _____ | _____ |
| LANGUAGE | 6/8 | _____ | _____ |
| TOTAL SCORE | 38/50 | _____ | _____ |

Were accommodations made in administering this test?   ❑ Yes   ❑ No

Type of accommodations: _____

_____

**DECODING**

**Sample**

**1.**

**2.**

**3.**

**4.**

GO ON

Harcourt • Reading and Language Skills Assessment

**DECODING:** (continued)

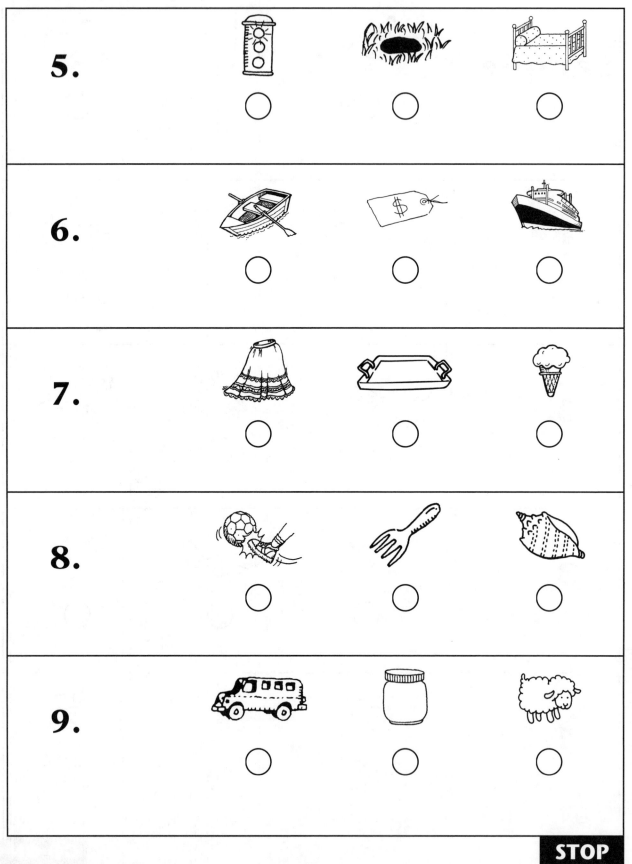

**STOP**

Mid-Year Skills

**DECODING:** (continued)

## Sample

pet        pat        pit

○        ○        ○

**10.**    ham    hat    hill

○        ○        ○

**11.**    mill    mitt    man

○        ○        ○

**12.**    cut    coat    cat

○        ○        ○

**GO ON**

Harcourt • Reading and Language Skills Assessment

**DECODING:** (continued)

**13.**  top ○    tip ○    tap ○

**14.**  mass ○    mess ○    miss ○

**15.**  not ○    net ○    nut ○

**16.**  horn ○    hot ○    hip ○

**GO ON** ▶

Harcourt • Reading and Language Skills Assessment

**DECODING:** (continued)

**17.**     ban     barn     bun
○     ○     ○

**18.**     bed     bad     bird
○     ○     ○

**STOP**

**DECODING:** (continued)

**Sample**
fr

**19.** sm

**20.** st

**21.** tr

**22.** cr

**GO ON** ▶

Harcourt • Reading and Language Skills Assessment

**DECODING:** (continued)

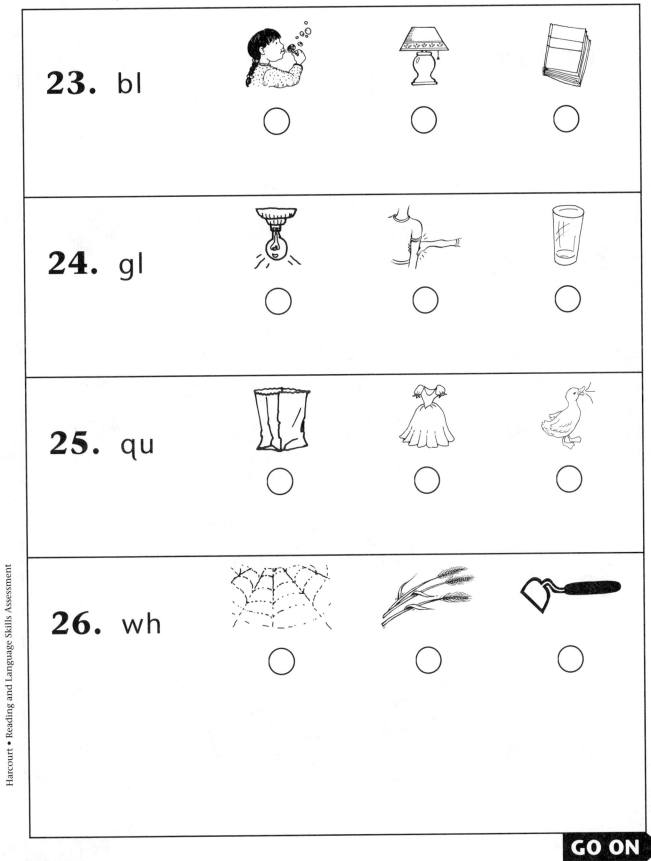

**23.** bl

        ◯        ◯        ◯

**24.** gl

        ◯        ◯        ◯

**25.** qu

        ◯        ◯        ◯

**26.** wh

        ◯        ◯        ◯

**GO ON ▶**

**DECODING:** (continued)

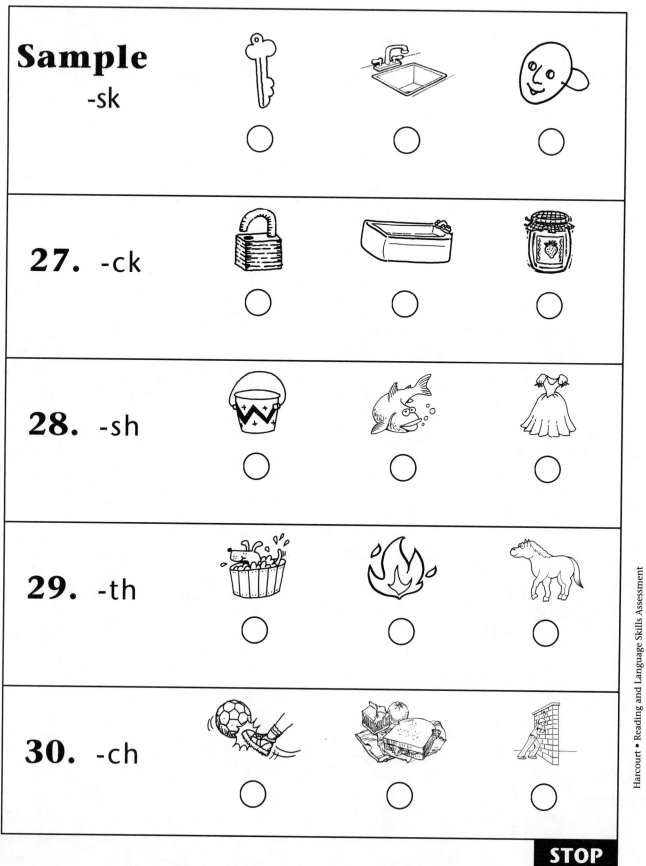

**Sample**
-sk

**27.** -ck

**28.** -sh

**29.** -th

**30.** -ch

Harcourt • Reading and Language Skills Assessment

**STOP**

Mid-Year Skills

**DECODING:** (continued)

## Sample

She _____ the box.

pack               packed               packing
○                    ○                    ○

**31.** The plant is _____.

grow               grows               growing
○                    ○                    ○

**32.** She _____ her drink.

spilled               spill               spilling
○                    ○                    ○

**GO ON**

**DECODING:** (continued)

**33.** Dan is _____a book.

read       reads       reading

○           ○           ○

**34.** She _____me pick up sticks.

help       helps       helping

○           ○           ○

**STOP**

**Score** _____

**COMPREHENSION**

# Sample

## Growing a Plant

Here is how to grow a plant.
Put the plant in the sun.
Give the plant a drink every day.
Watch the plant grow.

What should you do **first**?

○ Watch the plant grow.

○ Put the plant in the sun.

○ Give the plant a drink.

**GO ON**

**COMPREHENSION:** (continued)

# Tom Gets Up

It was a summer morning.
"It is time to get up, Tom,"
Mom said.
Tom jumped out of bed.
First, he got dressed.
Next, he drank a glass of milk.
He had some toast to eat, too.
Then, he got his bat and ball.
Last, Tom ran into the yard to play
ball with his friends.

**35.** When did this story take place?

    ○  in the morning

    ○  at night

    ○  at bed time

**COMPREHENSION:** (continued)

**36.** What did Mom tell Tom to do?
○ have toast
○ get up
○ play ball

**37.** What did Tom do **first**?
○ ran into the yard
○ drank milk
○ got dressed

**38.** Who will play with Tom?
○ Mom
○ his friends
○ Tom's sister

**GO ON**

**COMPREHENSION:** (continued)

# Kit and Ann Make a Snack

It was time to go to bed.

Kit and Ann wanted a snack to eat before bed.

Dad said, "You can make some toast."

First, Kit made some toast.

Then, Ann put jam on the toast.

Last, Kit and Ann sat down to eat their snack.

**39.** When did this story take place?

　○　in the morning

　○　at lunch

　○　at bed time

**COMPREHENSION:** (continued)

**40.** What did Kit and Ann want?
- ○ a book
- ○ a snack
- ○ a drink

**41.** Who put jam on the toast?
- ○ Ann
- ○ Kit
- ○ Dad

**42.** What did Kit and Ann do **last**?
- ○ They made some toast.
- ○ They put jam on the toast.
- ○ They sat down to eat their snack.

**STOP**

**LANGUAGE**

# Sample 1

my cat? Where is

Yes 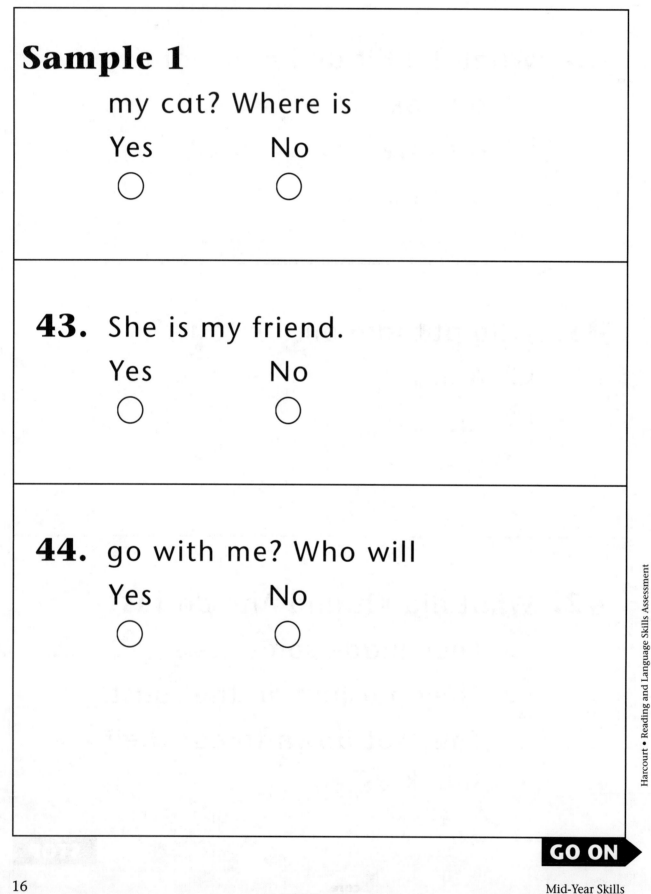          No
◯             ◯

**43.** She is my friend.

Yes          No
◯             ◯

**44.** go with me? Who will

Yes          No
◯             ◯

**LANGUAGE:** (continued)

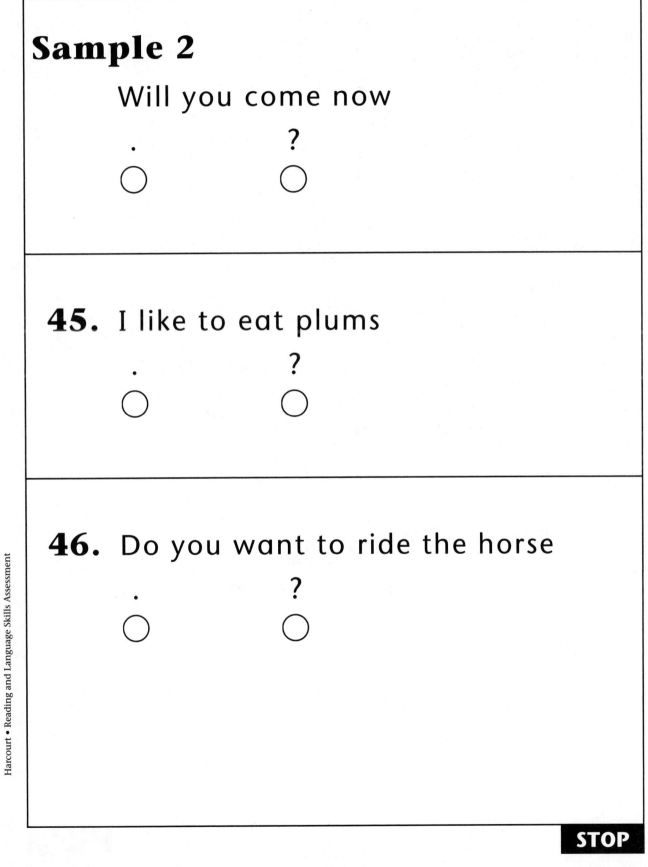

# Sample 2

Will you come now

.          ?
◯          ◯

---

**45.** I like to eat plums

.          ?
◯          ◯

---

**46.** Do you want to ride the horse

.          ?
◯          ◯

**STOP**

**LANGUAGE:** (continued)

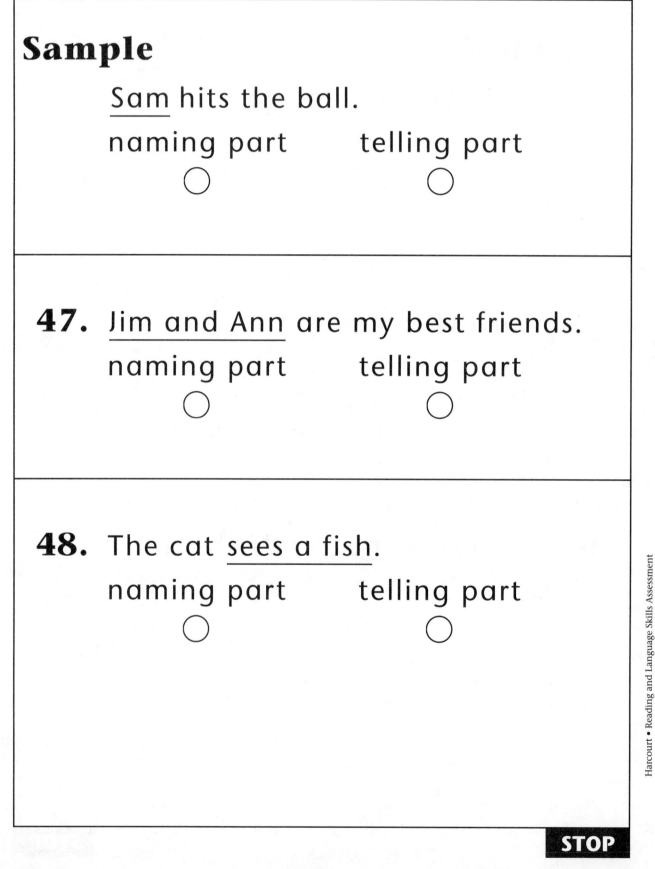

**Sample**

Sam hits the ball.

naming part        telling part
   ◯                   ◯

**47.** Jim and Ann are my best friends.

naming part        telling part
   ◯                   ◯

**48.** The cat sees a fish.

naming part        telling part
   ◯                   ◯

**STOP**

**LANGUAGE:** (continued)

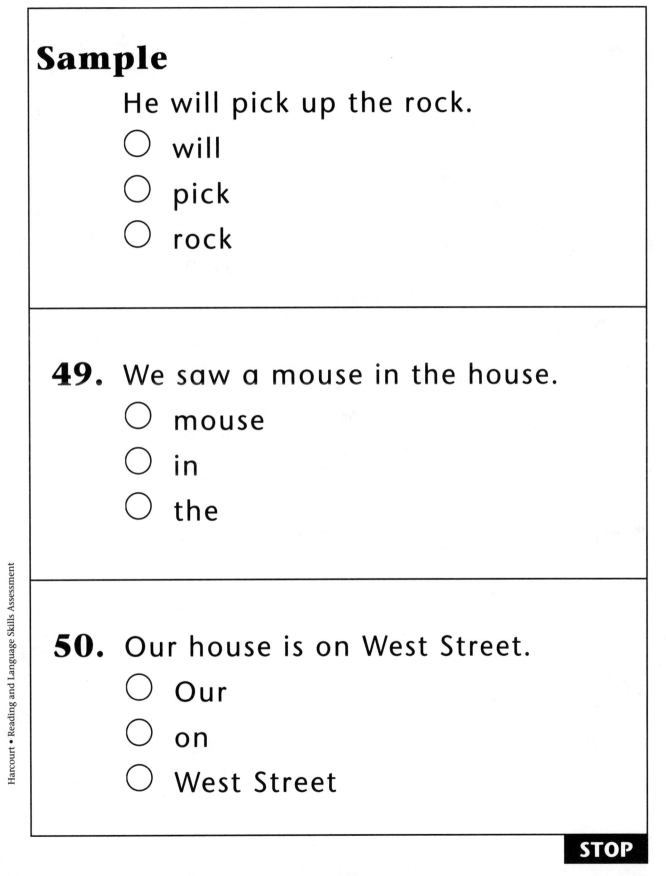

## Sample

He will pick up the rock.

○ will

○ pick

○ rock

**49.** We saw a mouse in the house.

○ mouse

○ in

○ the

**50.** Our house is on West Street.

○ Our

○ on

○ West Street

**STOP**

Harcourt • Reading and Language Skills Assessment

· T R O P H I E S ·

**Books 1-1, 1-2, 1-3**

**Reading and Language Skills Assessment**

Orlando   Boston   Dallas   Chicago   San Diego

Part No. 9997-37700-1

ISBN 0-15-332164-4  (Package of 12)

1-3

# TROPHIES

# Reading and Language Skills
# Assessment Pretest

## Time Together/Book 1-4

Name _____ Date _____

| SKILL AREA | Criterion Score | Pupil Score | Pupil Strength |
|---|---|---|---|
| **DECODING** | | | |
| Long Vowels /ē/e, ee, ea; /ā/a-e; /ī/i-e; /ō/o-e | | | |
| Decodable Words | 6/8 | _____ | _____ |
| Contractions: 's, n't, 'll | 3/4 | _____ | _____ |
| **VOCABULARY** | | | |
| Classify/Categorize | 3/4 | _____ | _____ |
| **RESEARCH AND INFORMATION SKILLS** | | | |
| Alphabetize | 3/4 | _____ | _____ |
| **LANGUAGE** | 6/8 | _____ | _____ |
| Using *I* and *Me* | | | |
| Using *He, She, It,* and *They* | | | |
| Describing Words: Feelings | | | |
| Describing Words: Color, Size, Shape | | | |
| Describing Words: Taste, Smell, Sound | | | |
| Describing Words: How Many | | | |
| Describing Words: Weather | | | |
| **TOTAL SCORE** | 21/28 | _____ | _____ |

Were accommodations made in administering this test?  ☐ Yes  ☐ No

Type of accommodations: _____

_____

**DECODING:** Vowels: Decodable Words

**Sample**

pale ○    pole ○    pile ○

1. shop ○    sheep ○    shape ○

2. ride ○    rod ○    read ○

3. spoke ○    speak ○    spike ○

4. bike ○    bake ○    buck ○

**GO ON**

**DECODING:** Vowels: Decodable Words (continued)

**5.**    skate   skit   skeet
   ○   ○   ○

**6.**   like   lake   luck
   ○   ○   ○

**7.**   dim   dame   dome
   ○   ○   ○

**8.**   male   mole   mile
   ○   ○   ○

**STOP**

Harcourt • Reading and Language Skills Assessment

**DECODING:** Contractions

**Sample**

I'll read the book to you.

I will ○          You will ○          We will ○

---

**9.** She'll ride my bike.

He will ○          She will ○          I will ○

---

**10.** Who's kicking the ball?

What is ○          Why is ○          Who is ○

---

**11.** Mother said, "Don't run!"

Do not ○          Will not ○          Is not ○

---

**12.** He's my friend.

He sees ○          He was ○          He is ○

**STOP**

**VOCABULARY:** Classify/Categorize

**Sample**

How are <u>cat</u>, <u>bird</u>, <u>dog</u> the **same**?

○ They are plants.

○ They are animals.

○ They are games.

13. How are <u>milk</u>, <u>water</u>, <u>tea</u> the **same**?

○ They are bugs.

○ They are sports.

○ They are drinks.

14. How are <u>bike</u>, <u>car</u>, <u>bus</u> the **same**?

○ They have wheels.

○ They have tails.

○ They have ears.

15. How are <u>toast</u>, <u>jam</u>, <u>plums</u> the **same**?

○ They are games to play.

○ They are foods to eat.

○ They are songs to sing.

**GO ON**

**VOCABULARY:** Classify/Categorize (continued)

**16.** How are <u>coat</u>, <u>skirt</u>, <u>shirt</u> the **same**?

○ They are things to put on.

○ They are things to throw.

○ They are things to plant.

**STOP**

**RESEARCH AND INFORMATION SKILLS:** Alphabetize

| | |
|---|---|
| **Sample** | ○ dog, pin, ant<br>○ ant, dog, pin |
| **17.** | ○ egg, lock, nose<br>○ nose, egg, lock |
| **18.** | ○ truck, wig, rose<br>○ rose, truck, wig |
| **19.** | ○ cream, fire, king<br>○ fire, cream, king |
| **20.** | ○ silk, vase, oak<br>○ oak, silk, vase |

**STOP**

**Score _____**

Harcourt • Reading and Language Skills Assessment

**LANGUAGE**

**Sample 1**

_____ reads a book.

He ○          It ○

**21.** Throw _____ to me.

he ○          it ○

**22.** _____ is making cookies.

She ○          It ○

**23.** _____ stand by Dad.

I ○          Me ○

**STOP**

**LANGUAGE** (continued)

**24.** _____ are playing a game.

She          They

○              ○

Harcourt • Reading and Language Skills Assessment

**GO ON** ▶

**LANGUAGE** (continued)

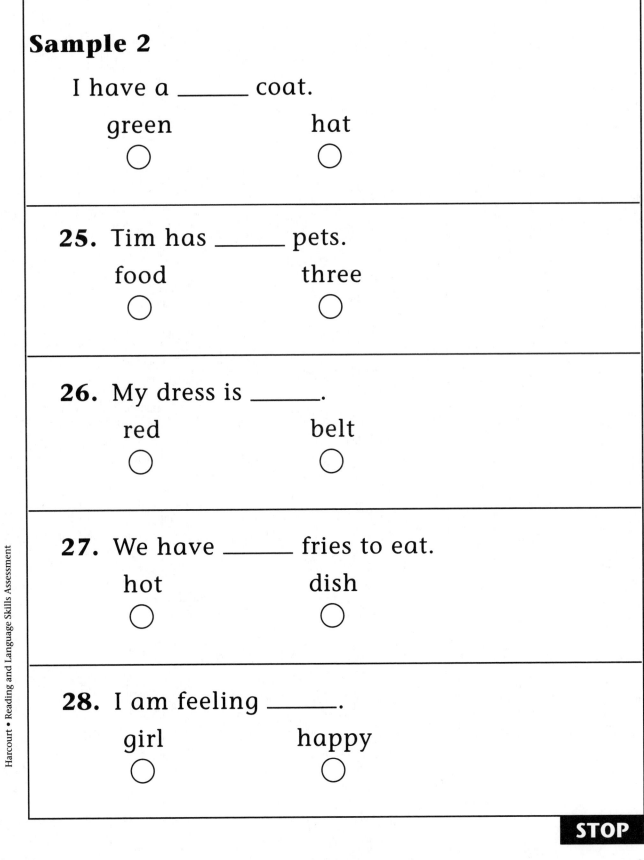

**Sample 2**

I have a _____ coat.

green ◯          hat ◯

**25.** Tim has _____ pets.

food ◯          three ◯

**26.** My dress is _____.

red ◯          belt ◯

**27.** We have _____ fries to eat.

hot ◯          dish ◯

**28.** I am feeling _____.

girl ◯          happy ◯

**STOP**

## TROPHIES

# Time Together/Book 1-4
## Reading and Language Skills Assessment

### Harcourt

Orlando   Boston   Dallas   Chicago   San Diego

Part No. 9997-37702-8

ISBN 0-15-332165-2  (Package of 12)

1-4

# · T R O P H I E S ·

# Reading and Language Skills
# Assessment Posttest

## Time Together/Book 1-4

Name _____ Date _____

| SKILL AREA | Criterion Score | Pupil Score | Pupil Strength |
|---|---|---|---|
| **DECODING** | | | |
| Long Vowels | | | |
| /ē/e, ee, ea; /ā/a-e; /ī/i-e; /ō/o-e | | | |
| Decodable Words | 6/8 | _____ | _____ |
| Contractions: 's, n't, 'll | 3/4 | _____ | _____ |
| **VOCABULARY** | | | |
| Classify/Categorize | 3/4 | _____ | _____ |
| **RESEARCH AND INFORMATION SKILLS** | | | |
| Alphabetize | 3/4 | _____ | _____ |
| **LANGUAGE** | 6/8 | _____ | _____ |
| Using *I* and *Me* | | | |
| Using *He, She, It,* and *They* | | | |
| Describing Words: Feelings | | | |
| Describing Words: Color, Size, Shape | | | |
| Describing Words: Taste, Smell, Sound | | | |
| Describing Words: How Many | | | |
| Describing Words: Weather | | | |
| **TOTAL SCORE** | 21/28 | _____ | _____ |

Were accommodations made in administering this test?   ❏ Yes   ❏ No

Type of accommodations: _____

_____

Harcourt • Reading and Language Skills Assessment

**DECODING:** Vowels: Decodable Words

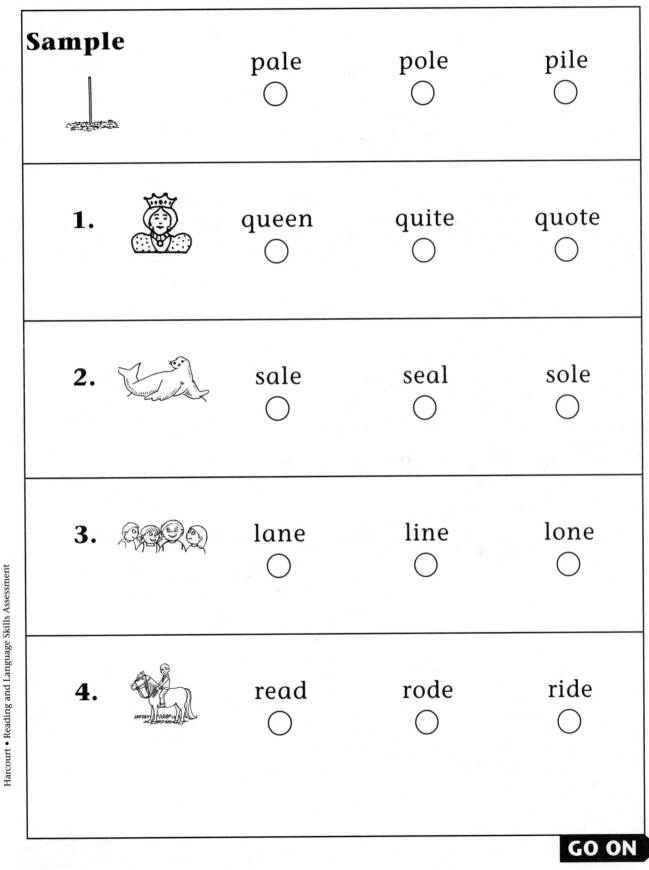

**Sample**

| pale | pole | pile |
| ○ | ○ | ○ |

**1.** 

| queen | quite | quote |
| ○ | ○ | ○ |

**2.**

| sale | seal | sole |
| ○ | ○ | ○ |

**3.**

| lane | line | lone |
| ○ | ○ | ○ |

**4.**

| read | rode | ride |
| ○ | ○ | ○ |

**GO ON**

Harcourt • Reading and Language Skills Assessment

**DECODING:** Vowels: Decodable Words (continued)

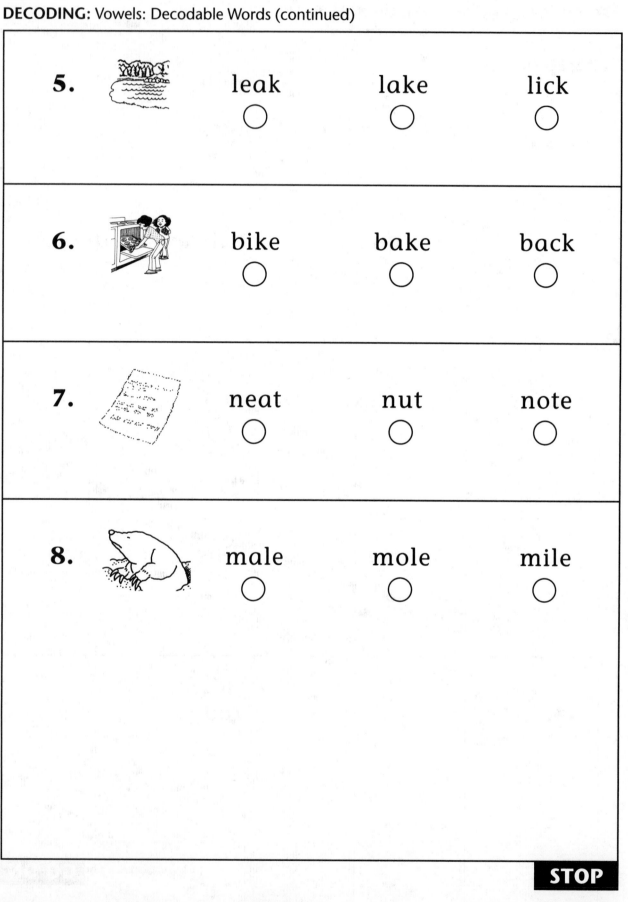

**5.**      leak          lake          lick
         ○           ○           ○

**6.**      bike          bake          back
         ○           ○           ○

**7.**      neat          nut          note
         ○           ○           ○

**8.**      male          mole          mile
         ○           ○           ○

**STOP**

**DECODING:** Contractions

**Sample**

I'll read the book to you.

I will          You will          We will
○                ○                ○

**9.** I can't open the door.

will not          can not          do not
○                ○                ○

**10.** Dad said, "Don't be late."

Is not          Do not          Will not
○                ○                ○

**11.** He's playing a game.

He sees          He was          He is
○                ○                ○

**12.** She'll make the bed.

She will          He will          I will
○                ○                ○

**STOP**

*Time Together / Book 1-4*          **Score** _____          3

**VOCABULARY:** Classify/Categorize

**Sample**

How are <u>cat</u>, <u>bird</u>, <u>dog</u> the **same**?

○ They are plants.

○ They are animals.

○ They are games.

**13.** How are <u>apple</u>, <u>banana</u>, <u>grape</u> the **same**?

○ They are bugs.

○ They are drinks.

○ They are foods.

**14.** How are <u>ant</u>, <u>bee</u>, <u>fly</u> the **same**?

○ They are songs.

○ They are insects.

○ They are games.

**15.** How are <u>lake</u>, <u>pond</u>, <u>stream</u> the **same**?

○ They have water.

○ They have hands.

○ They have legs.

**GO ON** ▶

Harcourt • Reading and Language Skills Assessment

*Time Together / Book 1-4*

**VOCABULARY:** Classify/Categorize (continued)

**16.** How are <u>tree</u>, <u>flower</u>, <u>shrub</u> the **same**?

○ They are plants.

○ They are drinks.

○ They are sports.

**STOP**

**RESEARCH AND INFORMATION SKILLS:** Alphabetize

**Sample**  ○ dog, pin, ant
○ ant, dog, pin

**17.**  ○ grass, hog, mice
○ mice, grass, hog

**18.**  ○ trap, inch, step
○ inch, step, trap

**19.**  ○ Dave, Jan, Carl
○ Carl, Dave, Jan

**20.**  ○ pet, ranch, wig
○ wig, pet, ranch

**STOP**

**Score** _____  *Time Together / Book 1-4*

Harcourt • Reading and Language Skills Assessment

**LANGUAGE**

**Sample 1**

\_\_\_\_\_ reads a book.

He ⚪   It ⚪

**21.** \_\_\_\_\_ are baking cookies.

They ⚪   It ⚪

**22.** \_\_\_\_\_ throw the ball to Rob.

Me ⚪   I ⚪

**23.** \_\_\_\_\_ is my dad.

He ⚪   She ⚪

**GO ON**

**LANGUAGE** (continued)

**24.** _____ is a fun game.

He                    It

○                    ○

**GO ON**

**LANGUAGE** (continued)

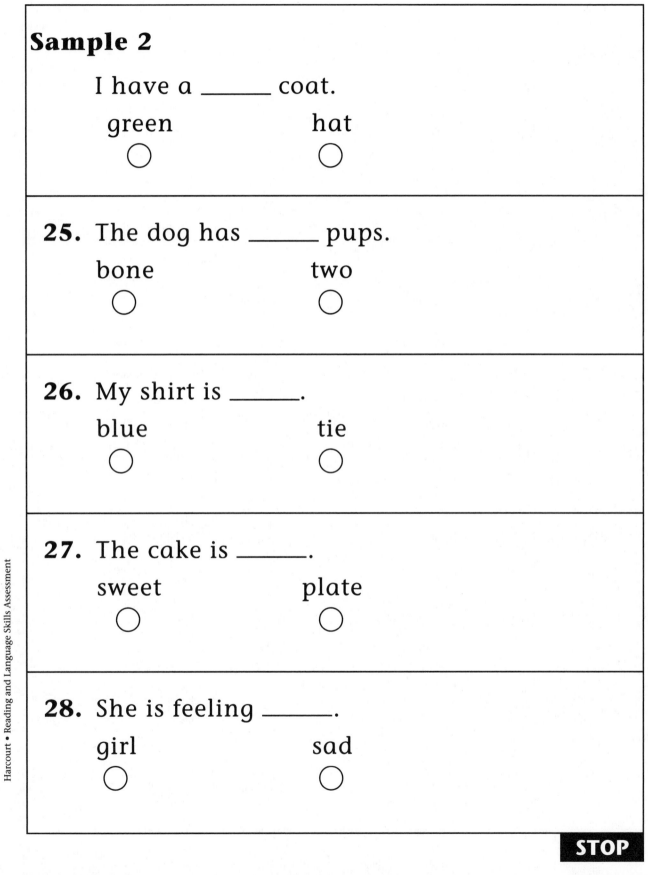

**Sample 2**

I have a _____ coat.

green    hat
○        ○

**25.** The dog has _____ pups.

bone     two
○        ○

**26.** My shirt is _____.

blue     tie
○        ○

**27.** The cake is _____.

sweet    plate
○        ○

**28.** She is feeling _____.

girl     sad
○        ○

**STOP**

Harcourt • Reading and Language Skills Assessment

• T R O P H I E S •

# Time Together/Book 1-4
## Reading and Language Skills Assessment

**Harcourt**

Orlando   Boston   Dallas   Chicago   San Diego

Part No. 9997-37703-6

ISBN 0-15-332165-2  (Package of 12)

1-4

# • T R O P H I E S •

# Reading and Language Skills Assessment Pretest

## Gather Around/Book 1-5

Name _____ Date _____

| SKILL AREA | Criterion Score | Pupil Score | Pupil Strength |
|---|---|---|---|
| **DECODING** | | | |
| Long Vowels /i/igh; /a/ai, ay; /oo̅/u-e | | | |
| Decodable Words | 4/6 | _____ | _____ |
| Inflections -ed, -ing (with spelling changes) | 3/4 | _____ | _____ |
| Contractions 've, 'd, 're | 3/4 | _____ | _____ |
| | | | |
| **COMPREHENSION** | | | |
| Plot | 3/4 | _____ | _____ |
| Main Idea | 3/4 | _____ | _____ |
| | | | |
| **LANGUAGE** | 4/6 | _____ | _____ |
| Verbs | | | |
| Verbs That Tell About Now | | | |
| Verbs That Tell About the Past | | | |
| | | | |
| **TOTAL SCORE** | 20/28 | _____ | _____ |

Were accommodations made in administering this test?  ☐ Yes  ☐ No

Type of accommodations: _____

ISBN 0-15-332174-1

8 9 10   170   10 09 08 07 06 05 04

**DECODING:** Vowels: Decodable Words

| **Sample** | | neat ◯ | night ◯ | note ◯ |
|---|---|---|---|---|
| **1.** | | null ◯ | nil ◯ | nail ◯ |
| **2.** | | hay ◯ | hoe ◯ | high ◯ |
| **3.** | | let ◯ | late ◯ | light ◯ |
| **4.** | | fleet ◯ | flight ◯ | float ◯ |
| **5.** | | mule ◯ | mile ◯ | mail ◯ |
| **6.** | | preen ◯ | prune ◯ | prone ◯ |

**STOP**

**DECODING:** Inflections

## Sample

My team is _____ the game.

win ○          wins ○          winning ○

---

**7.** The dog was _____ fast.

running ○          runs ○          run ○

---

**8.** The school bus _____ by the house.

stop ○          stopping ○          stopped ○

---

**9.** We are _____ the bus.

ride ○          riding ○          rides ○

---

**10.** Mom has _____ a pie.

baked ○          bakes ○          bake ○

**STOP**

Harcourt • Reading and Language Skills Assessment

**DECODING:** Contractions

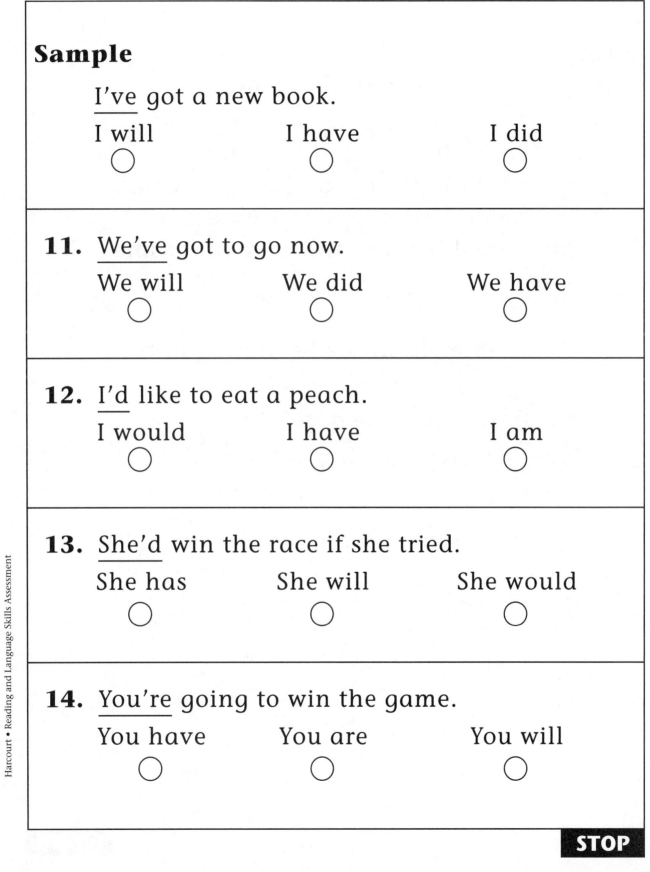

**Sample**

I've got a new book.
~~I've~~

I will          I have          I did
○              ○              ○

---

11. We've got to go now.
    ~~We've~~

   We will          We did          We have
   ○               ○               ○

---

12. I'd like to eat a peach.
    ~~I'd~~

   I would          I have          I am
   ○               ○               ○

---

13. She'd win the race if she tried.
    ~~She'd~~

   She has          She will          She would
   ○               ○               ○

---

14. You're going to win the game.
    ~~You're~~

   You have          You are          You will
   ○               ○               ○

**STOP**

**COMPREHENSION:** Plot

**Sample**

### Carl Finds a Dog

Carl saw a little dog in the yard.
He called to the dog, and the dog came.
The dog looked happy to see Carl.
Carl petted the dog and gave him some
water.

What happens at the beginning of this
story?

○ Carl petted the dog.

○ Carl gave the dog water.

○ Carl saw a dog in the yard.

**GO ON** ▶

**COMPREHENSION:** Plot (continued)

## The Fox and the Hens

The hens on a farm were upset.
They saw a fox near their house.
"The fox might eat us!" yelled an old
red hen.
"Let's cluck and crow," said a black hen.
"Farmer Bob will hear us. He will chase the
fox away."
The plan worked. The fox ran away.
Late that night, the fox came back. The red
hen saw the fox.
She yelled, "Fox!"
All the hens ran at the fox. They pecked
him all over.
The fox left and never came back.

**15.** What happens at the beginning of this
story?

○ Farmer Bob chases a fox.

○ The hens on a farm are upset.

○ A red hen yells "Fox!"

**GO ON**

**16.** Who do the hens think will eat them?

○ a fox

○ Farmer Bob

○ a crow

**17.** What happens after the fox runs away?

○ The hens cannot sleep.

○ The fox comes back late at night.

○ The fox takes the black hen's eggs.

**18.** How does the story end?

○ Farmer Bob catches the fox.

○ The fox leaves and does not come back.

○ The fox and the hens become friends.

**STOP**

**Score** _____

Harcourt • Reading and Language Skills Assessment

**COMPREHENSION:** Main Idea

**Sample**

## Going to School

Rose likes school.
She has a lot of friends there.
She reads books at school.
She plays games.
She learns so much.

What is this story mostly about?

○ Rose likes school.

○ Rose reads books at school.

○ Rose plays games.

**GO ON**

## A Sweet Treat

Bess made a cake.
She mixed some eggs and milk in a bowl.
Then, Bess added the cake mix.
When it was all mixed up, she put it in
a pan.
She baked the cake a long time.
Then, Bess ate a slice of the cake.

**19.** What is this story mostly about?
- ○ Bess added the cake mix.
- ○ Bess made a cake.
- ○ Bess ate a slice of the cake.

Harcourt • Reading and Language Skills Assessment

**COMPREHENSION:** Main Idea (continued)

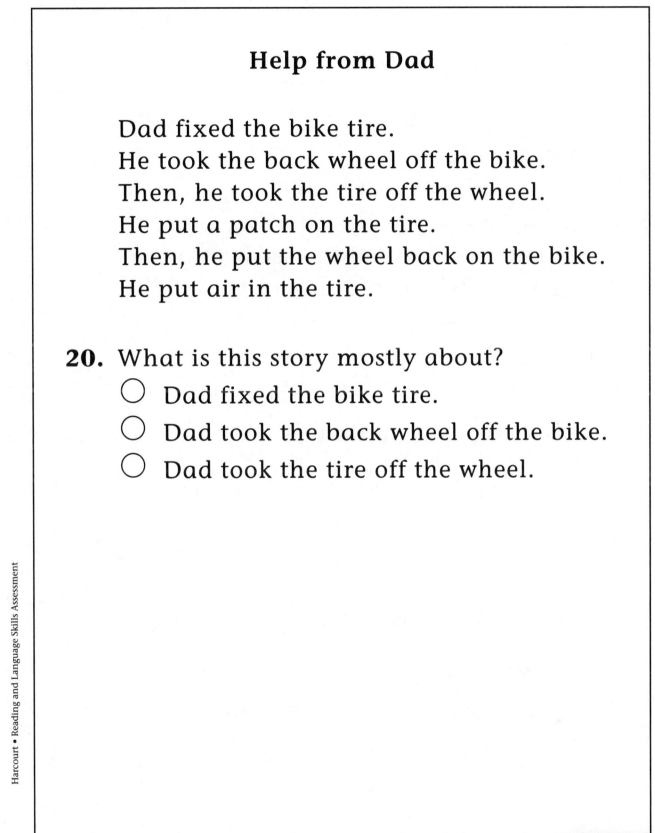

# Help from Dad

Dad fixed the bike tire.
He took the back wheel off the bike.
Then, he took the tire off the wheel.
He put a patch on the tire.
Then, he put the wheel back on the bike.
He put air in the tire.

**20.** What is this story mostly about?
   ○ Dad fixed the bike tire.
   ○ Dad took the back wheel off the bike.
   ○ Dad took the tire off the wheel.

**GO ON**

**COMPREHENSION:** Main Idea (continued)

## Planting Time

Les and Jen planted seeds.
They raked the dirt.
They made small rows.
They put seeds in each row.
Then they pushed the seeds into the dirt.
Last, they watered the seeds.

**21.** What is this story mostly about?

○ Les and Jen raked the dirt.

○ Les and Jen planted seeds.

○ Les and Jen watered the seeds.

*Gather Around* / Book 1-5

Harcourt • Reading and Language Skills Assessment

**COMPREHENSION:** Main Idea (continued)

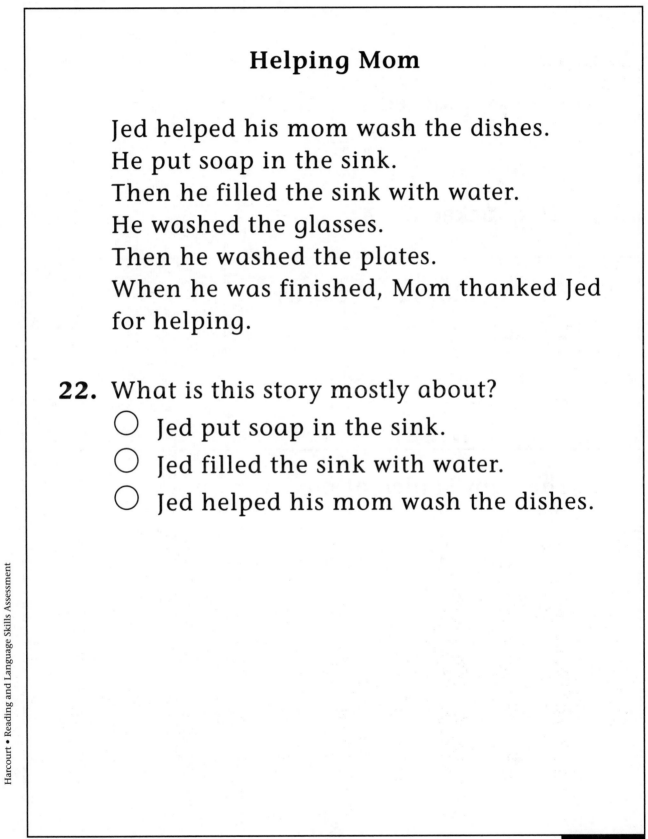

## Helping Mom

Jed helped his mom wash the dishes.
He put soap in the sink.
Then he filled the sink with water.
He washed the glasses.
Then he washed the plates.
When he was finished, Mom thanked Jed
for helping.

**22.** What is this story mostly about?
- ○ Jed put soap in the sink.
- ○ Jed filled the sink with water.
- ○ Jed helped his mom wash the dishes.

**STOP**

**LANGUAGE**: Verbs

**Sample**

Two ducks quacked.
- ○ Two
- ○ ducks
- ○ quacked

**23.** The cat plays in the grass.
- ○ cat
- ○ plays
- ○ grass

**24.** The baby smiled at me.
- ○ The
- ○ baby
- ○ smiled

**25.** Dad drives a red truck.
- ○ Dad
- ○ drives
- ○ red

Harcourt • Reading and Language Skills Assessment

**LANGUAGE:** Verbs (continued)

---

**26.** Tom and I are happy.

○ Tom

○ are

○ happy

---

**27.** My mom fills my glass with milk.

○ My

○ mom

○ fills

---

**28.** I jumped into the water.

○ jumped

○ into

○ water

---

**STOP**

　　　**Score** _____

· T R O P H I E S ·

# Gather Around/Book 1-5
# Reading and Language Skills Assessment

**Harcourt**

Orlando   Boston   Dallas   Chicago   San Diego

Part No. 9997-37705-2

ISBN 0-15-332174-1  (Package of 12)

1-5

# Reading and Language Skills
# Assessment Posttest

## Gather Around/Book 1-5

Name _____ Date _____

| SKILL AREA | Criterion Score | Pupil Score | Pupil Strength |
|---|---|---|---|
| **DECODING** | | | |
| Long Vowels /i/igh; /a/ai, ay; /o͞o/u-e | | | |
| Decodable Words | 4/6 | _____ | _____ |
| Inflections -ed, -ing (with spelling changes) | 3/4 | _____ | _____ |
| Contractions 've, 'd, 're | 3/4 | _____ | _____ |
| | | | |
| **COMPREHENSION** | | | |
| Plot | 3/4 | _____ | _____ |
| Main Idea | 3/4 | _____ | _____ |
| | | | |
| **LANGUAGE** | 4/6 | _____ | _____ |
| Verbs | | | |
| Verbs That Tell About Now | | | |
| Verbs That Tell About the Past | | | |
| | | | |
| **TOTAL SCORE** | 20/28 | _____ | _____ |

Were accommodations made in administering this test?   ☐ Yes   ☐ No

Type of accommodations: _____

**DECODING: Vowels:** Decodable Words

## Sample

|  | neat ○ | night ○ | note ○ |

**1.** RED | pint ○ | punt ○ | paint ○ |

**2.** | tree ○ | tray ○ | truce ○ |

**3.** | right ○ | rat ○ | rot ○ |

**4.** | let ○ | late ○ | light ○ |

GO ON

**DECODING: Vowels:** Decodable Words (continued)

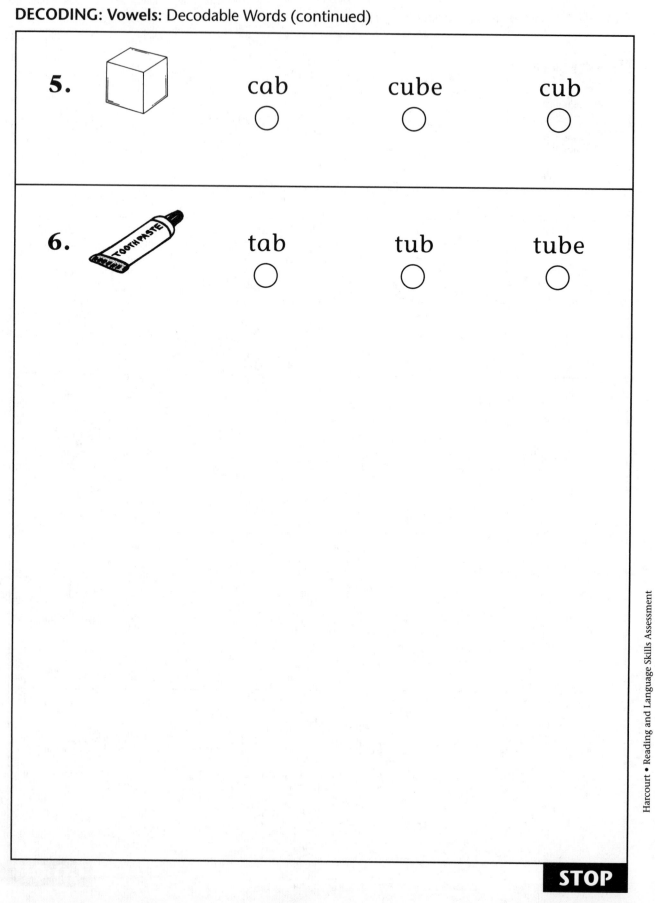

**5.**    cab          cube          cub
         ○            ○            ○

**6.**    tab          tub          tube
         ○            ○            ○

**STOP**

**Score** _____          *Gather Around / Book 1-5*

Harcourt • Reading and Language Skills Assessment

**DECODING:** Inflections

**Sample**

My team is _____ the game.

win          wins          winning
○              ○              ○

7. The baby is _____ her hands.

clapping      claps        clapped
○              ○              ○

8. She _____ and fell down.

slip          slipped      slipping
○              ○              ○

9. I am _____ from my friend.

hide          hides        hiding
○              ○              ○

10. We _____ up for lunch.

lined          lines        lining
○              ○              ○

**STOP**

**DECODING:** Contractions

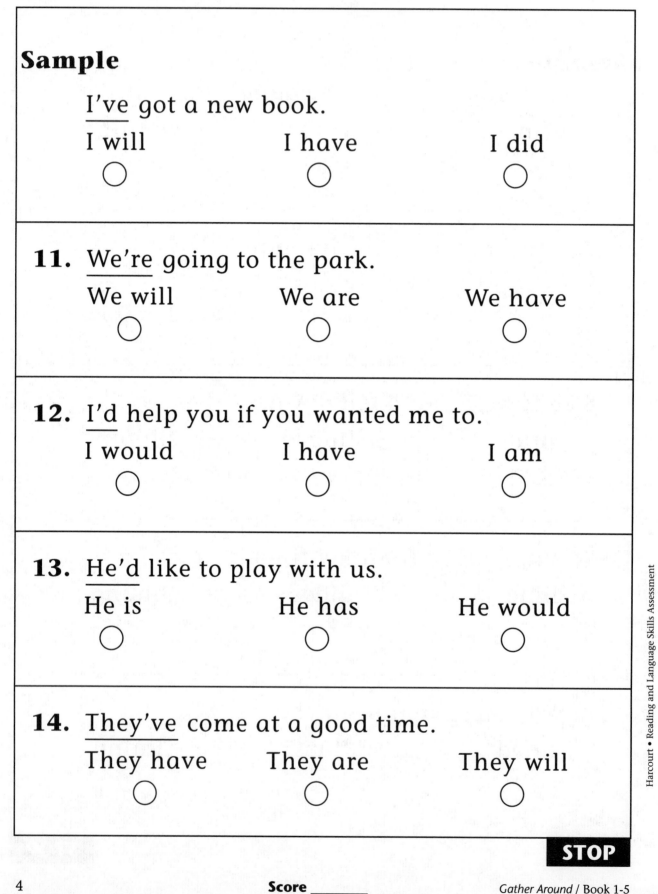

**Sample**

I've got a new book.

I will          I have          I did
○               ○               ○

**11.** We're going to the park.

We will          We are          We have
○                ○               ○

**12.** I'd help you if you wanted me to.

I would          I have          I am
○                ○               ○

**13.** He'd like to play with us.

He is          He has          He would
○              ○               ○

**14.** They've come at a good time.

They have          They are          They will
○                  ○                ○

**STOP**

**Score** _____          *Gather Around / Book 1-5*

Harcourt • Reading and Language Skills Assessment

**COMPREHENSION:** Plot

## Sample

### Carl Finds a Dog

Carl saw a little dog in the yard.
He called to the dog, and the dog came.
The dog looked happy to see Carl.
Carl petted the dog and gave him some
water.

What happens at the beginning of this story?

○  Carl petted the dog.

○  Carl gave the dog water.

○  Carl saw a dog in the yard.

**GO ON**

**COMPREHENSION:** Plot (continued)

### Tip and Tom Cat

Tip wanted to be big and strong.
But he was the smallest pup on his block.
When Tom Cat came by, Tip barked and barked.
Tom Cat just walked by.
Tip's mom said, "Do not worry. Every day you will get bigger."
Time went by. All winter Tip ate good food.
He ran and jumped.
He got big and strong.
One spring day, Tom Cat came by. Tip barked and growled at Tom.
Tom Cat ran away as fast as he could run.

**15.** What is Tip's problem in this story?
- ○ Tip wants out of the yard.
- ○ Tip has no friends to play with.
- ○ Tip wants to be big and strong.

Harcourt • Reading and Language Skills Assessment

**COMPREHENSION:** Plot (continued)

**16.** Who does Tip bark at?
- ○ his mom
- ○ Tom Cat
- ○ other dogs

**17.** What happens in the winter?
- ○ Tip gets big and strong.
- ○ Tom goes away.
- ○ Tip's mom has pups.

**18.** How does the story end?
- ○ Tom Cat runs away when Tip barks.
- ○ Tom Cat and Tip become friends.
- ○ Tip's mom chases Tom away.

**STOP**

**COMPREHENSION:** Main Idea

**Sample**

## Going to School

Rose likes school.
She has a lot of friends there.
She reads books at school.
She plays games.
She learns so much.

What is this story mostly about?
○ Rose likes school.
○ Rose reads books at school.
○ Rose plays games.

**COMPREHENSION:** Main Idea (continued)

# Making a Kite

Dad helped Rob make a kite.
Rob got a big trash bag.
Dad cut the bag into a pretty shape.
They glued two sticks to the bag.
Dad put a string on the kite.
Then they went out to fly the kite.

**19.** What is this story mostly about?

○ Rob got a big trash bag.

○ Dad helped Rob make a kite.

○ Dad and Rob glued two sticks to the bag.

**GO ON** ▶

## Cards for Mom

Tonya and Kim made cards for Mom.
They got crayons and paper.
Then, they colored pictures.
Tonya put a red rose on her card.
Kim put a big star on her card.
Last, they gave the cards to Mom.

**20.** What is this story mostly about?

○ Tonya put a red rose on her card.

○ Kim put a big star on her card.

○ Tonya and Kim made cards for Mom.

Harcourt • Reading and Language Skills Assessment

**COMPREHENSION:** Main Idea (continued)

# Doing Things with Grandpa

Grandpa and I like to do things together.
Sometimes we read books.
Sometimes we go for a walk.
We even go fishing now and then.
I want to be just like Grandpa when I
grow up.

**21.** What is this story mostly about?

○ Grandpa and I like to do things
together.

○ Sometimes we go for a walk.

○ We go fishing now and then.

**GO ON**

# Helping at Home

I help at home in many ways.
I make my bed every day.
I give our dog food and water.
I keep my room clean.
I even take out the trash sometimes.
It is fun to be a helper.


**22.** What is this story mostly about?

    ◯  I make my bed every day.

    ◯  I help at home in many ways.

    ◯  I keep my room clean.

Harcourt • Reading and Language Skills Assessment

**LANGUAGE:** Verbs

**Sample**

Two ducks quacked.

○ Two

○ ducks

○ quacked

---

**23.** The dog chases the cat.

○ dog

○ chases

○ cat

---

**24.** The girls played a game.

○ The

○ girls

○ played

---

**25.** Dan ripped his new shirt.

○ Dan

○ ripped

○ shirt

**GO ON**

**LANGUAGE:** Verbs (continued)

**26.** Jess is lucky.

○ Jess

○ is

○ lucky

**27.** Jack's dad throws the ball to him.

○ Jack's

○ dad

○ throws

**28.** She hiked down the path.

○ hiked

○ the

○ path

**STOP**

Harcourt • Reading and Language Skills Assessment

· T R O P H I E S ·

# Gather Around/Book 1-5
## Reading and Language Skills Assessment

**Harcourt**

Orlando    Boston    Dallas    Chicago    San Diego

Part No. 9997-37706-0

ISBN 0-15-332174-1  (Package of 12)

1-5

# TROPHIES

# End-of-Year Reading and Language Skills Assessment

## Books 1-1—1-5

Name_____ Date_____

| SKILL AREA | Criterion Score | Pupil Score | Comments |
|---|---|---|---|
| DECODING/PHONICS | 16/22 | _____ | _____ |
| VOCABULARY | 3/4 | _____ | _____ |
| RESEARCH AND INFORMATION SKILLS | 3/4 | _____ | _____ |
| | | _____ | _____ |
| COMPREHENSION | 6/8 | | |
| LANGUAGE | 7/10 | _____ | _____ |
| TOTAL SCORE | 35/48 | _____ | _____ |

Were accommodations made in administering this test?  ❑ Yes  ❑ No

Type of accommodations: _____

_____

ISBN 0-15-332174-1

8 9 10   170   10 09 08 07 06 05 04

Harcourt • Reading and Language Skills Assessment

**DECODING**

# Sample

| | pale | pole | pile |
|---|---|---|---|
| | ○ | ○ | ○ |

**1.** | shop | sheep | shape |
|---|---|---|---|
| ○ | ○ | ○ |

**2.** | ride | road | read |
|---|---|---|---|
| ○ | ○ | ○ |

**3.** | skate | skit | skeet |
|---|---|---|---|
| ○ | ○ | ○ |

**4.** | null | nil | nail |
|---|---|---|---|
| ○ | ○ | ○ |

**GO ON**

**DECODING** (continued)

**5.**  hay ○     how ○     high ○

**6.**  let ○     late ○     light ○

**7.**  dim ○     dame ○     dome ○

**8.**  bike ○     bake ○     buck ○

**GO ON** ▶

**DECODING** (continued)

9.  preen ○   prune ○   prone ○

10.  crow ○   crib ○   crab ○

11.  ban ○   barn ○   bun ○

12.  third ○   thud ○   that ○

**STOP**

Harcourt • Reading and Language Skills Assessment

**DECODING** (continued)

**Sample**

My favorite team is _____ the game.

| win | wins | winning |
|:---:|:---:|:---:|
| ○ | ○ | ○ |

**13.** The happy baby was _____ at me.

| grinning | grins | grin |
|:---:|:---:|:---:|
| ○ | ○ | ○ |

**14.** She _____ her sore knee.

| rub | rubbed | rubbing |
|:---:|:---:|:---:|
| ○ | ○ | ○ |

**15.** When are you _____ to see us?

| come | coming | comes |
|:---:|:---:|:---:|
| ○ | ○ | ○ |

**16.** We have just _____ here.

| moved | moves | moving |
|:---:|:---:|:---:|
| ○ | ○ | ○ |

**STOP**

Harcourt • Reading and Language Skills Assessment

**DECODING** (continued)

**Sample**

I'll read the book to you.

I will                    You will                    We will

○                         ○                         ○

17. He'll ride on the bus.

He will                    She will                    I will

○                         ○                         ○

18. Dad said, "Don't yell!"

Do not                    Will not                    Is not

○                         ○                         ○

19. She's going to school.

She will                    She did                    She is

○                         ○                         ○

**GO ON**

**DECODING** (continued)

**20.** <u>You've</u> got a good pet.

You will          You have          You did

○                    ○                    ○

**21.** <u>She'd</u> like to play with you.

She does          She has          She would

○                    ○                    ○

**22.** <u>You're</u> going to run in a race.

You have          You are          You will

○                    ○                    ○

**STOP**

**Score** _____          End-of-Year Skills

Harcourt • Reading and Language Skills Assessment

**VOCABULARY**

## Sample

How are <u>cat</u>, <u>bird</u>, <u>dog</u> the **same**?
- ○ They are plants.
- ○ They are animals.
- ○ They are games.

**23.** How are <u>nuts</u>, <u>beans</u>, <u>apples</u> the **same**?
- ○ They are bugs.
- ○ They are foods.
- ○ They are drinks.

**24.** How are <u>stars</u>, <u>sun</u>, <u>moon</u> the **same**?
- ○ They are things in the sky.
- ○ They are things to plant.
- ○ They are things to eat.

**25.** How are <u>crab</u>, <u>fish</u>, <u>shark</u> the **same**?
- ○ They live in the dirt.
- ○ They live in the trees.
- ○ They live in the water.

**GO ON**

**VOCABULARY** (continued)

**26.** How are <u>cap</u>, <u>belt</u>, <u>dress</u> the **same**?
- ○ They are things to put on.
- ○ They are things to throw.
- ○ They are things to plant.

**RESEARCH AND INFORMATION SKILLS**

**Sample**  ○ dog, pin, ant
○ ant, dog, pin

**27.**  ○ fox, leg, nest
○ nest, fox, leg

**28.**  ○ tub, when, race
○ race, tub, when

**29.**  ○ cage, fight, jar
○ fight, jar, cage

**30.**  ○ step, vest, ostrich
○ ostrich, step, vest

**STOP**

Harcourt • Reading and Language Skills Assessment

**COMPREHENSION**

## Sample

### Carl Finds a Dog

Carl saw a little dog in the yard.
He called to the dog, and the dog came.
The dog looked happy to see Carl.
Carl petted the dog and gave him some
water.

What happens at the beginning of this story?

○ Carl petted the dog.

○ Carl gave the dog water.

○ Carl saw a dog in the yard.

**COMPREHENSION** (continued)

## Pete's Day in the Country

Pete was reading a book about animals.
"I wish I could see some animals," he said.
Mom said, "Let's go for a drive in the country, then."
Mom and Pete saw many animals on their drive.
First, they saw some deer by a stream.
Then they saw some squirrels up in a tree.
They even saw a horse crossing the road!
When they got home, Pete ran inside to tell Dad what they saw.

**31.** What does Pete want to do?
- ○ color pictures
- ○ see animals
- ○ play outside

**32.** Where does Pete go?
- ○ to the country
- ○ to a farm
- ○ to school

**GO ON**

**COMPREHENSION** (continued)

**33.** Who goes on the drive with Pete?

○ Mom

○ Dad

○ a friend

**34.** What does Pete see **first**?

○ some squirrels

○ some deer

○ a horse

**35.** What does Pete see crossing the road?

○ some squirrels

○ some deer

○ a horse

**36.** What happens at the end of the story?

○ Pete runs to tell Dad what they saw.

○ Mom says they will go see more animals.

○ Pete gets a new pet to keep at home.

**STOP**

Harcourt • Reading and Language Skills Assessment

**COMPREHENSION** (continued)

## Sample

### Going to School

Rose likes school.
She has a lot of friends there.
She reads books at school, and she plays games.
She learns so much.

What is this story mostly about?
- ○ Rose likes school.
- ○ Rose reads books at school.
- ○ Rose plays games.

**GO ON**

## Kinds of Fish

There are many kinds of fish.
There are goldfish.
There are red fish.
There are even rainbow fish!
It is fun to look at fish.

**37.** What is this story mostly about?
- ○ There are goldfish.
- ○ There are red fish.
- ○ There are many kinds of fish.

**COMPREHENSION** (continued)

## Caring for a Puppy

You should take good care of a puppy.
You should give a puppy water, and you
should give it puppy food.
You should play with a puppy every day.

**38.** What is this story mostly about?
- ○ You should take good care of a puppy.
- ○ You should give a puppy water.
- ○ You should give a puppy food.

**STOP**

**LANGUAGE**

**Sample**

He will pick up the rock.

- ○ will
- ○ pick
- ○ rock

---

**39.** Dick will feed the dog now.

- ○ will
- ○ dog
- ○ now

---

**40.** Dr. Frank lives by me.

- ○ Dr. Frank
- ○ lives
- ○ by

Harcourt • Reading and Language Skills Assessment

**LANGUAGE** (continued)

## Sample

_____ reads a book.

He
○

It
○

---

**41.** _____ will give me a pet to care for.

He
○

She
○

---

**42.** _____ are eating lunch together.

She
○

They
○

**STOP**

**LANGUAGE** (continued)

**Sample**

I have a _____ coat.

green            hat
○               ○

**43.** That bug has _____ legs.

nose          six
○            ○

**44.** The water feels _____ on my skin.

cold         drink
○           ○

**45.** It was a gray and _____ day.

rainy       water
○           ○

**46.** I feel very _____.

lunch       hungry
○           ○

**STOP**

Harcourt • Reading and Language Skills Assessment

**LANGUAGE** (continued)

## Sample

Two ducks quacked.

○ Two

○ ducks

○ quacked

---

**47.** Mary and Jane ran up the hill.

○ Jane

○ ran

○ hill

---

**48.** My friends are fun to play with.

○ My

○ friends

○ are

· TROPHIES ·

**End-of-Year Reading and Language Skills
Assessment/ Books 1-1—1-5**
**Reading and Language Skills Assessment**

Harcourt

Orlando   Boston   Dallas   Chicago   San Diego

Part No. 9997-37707-9

ISBN 0-15-332174-1  (Package of 12)

1-5